The Scented

VICTORIAN GARDEN

Family
LIBRARY

The List of Guests

THE SCENTED
VICTORIAN GARDEN

Australian
Household
Companion

THIS BOOK BELONGS TO

Celia Bowtell

30th September, 1993

(xxxx mum.)

Foreword

THE AUSTRALIAN HOUSEHOLD COMPANION is a collection of well-loved, traditional Australian recipes and old-fashioned household wisdom.

This charming little volume will evoke a bygone era, when our grandmothers and great-grandmothers had a store of useful knowledge, much of which has been lost in today's busy modern world.

The contents are strictly practical; the recipes are nourishing and tasty family fare. While the pioneers may have eaten roast emu, boiled bandicoot and parrot pie, such dishes will not be found in this book. All ingredients, as well as weights and measures, have been updated to modern equivalents.

The household hints, health and beauty secrets and natural remedies offer tried and true advice, giving safe and inexpensive alternatives to the hi-tech products of today. Some of the ingredients may be a little unfamiliar, but all are obtainable from chemists, hardware shops, craft or hobby shops, health food stores or even supermarkets.

Your own household tips and recipes may be added, and the book will be used and treasured for many years.

Contents

Recipes from Grandmother's Kitchen

Soups

HOTCH-POTCH

3 onions, 3 carrots, herbs, 1 cabbage, 1 cup peas,
1 cauliflower, 2 turnips, 1 teaspoon sugar, salt,
8 peppercorns, 3–4 potatoes, 3 litres water.

PREPARE ALL THE VEGETABLES and spices, and put them on to simmer until tender in 3 litres of water. Strain and sieve or blend until smooth. Return to the stock and add the seasoning and milk. Let the mixture simmer gently until ready to serve. Place a few slices of toast in a soup tureen and pour the mixture over them.

CARROT SOUP

1 kg washed carrots, 125 g butter, salt, cayenne,
2.5 litres stock.

SLICE THE CARROTS and put them in a saucepan with the butter, salt and cayenne. Stew gently until soft, then add the stock and simmer until the carrots are soft enough to sieve (or use a blender). Skim off any scum.
Optional: for a less sweet soup, add a parsnip and an onion.

BENDIGO SOUP

1 cauliflower, 500 g onions, 30 g butter, bacon bones,
salt and pepper, 2 cups milk.

BREAK THE CAULIFLOWER into flowerets. Cook in boiling salted water for 10 minutes, then strain. Peel and slice the onions, put them in a saucepan and cook them in oil for 5 minutes. Add the bacon bones, cauliflower, seasonings and 4 cups of water. Bring to the boil and simmer for 30 minutes. Remove the bones and sieve or blend the rest of the mixture. Add the milk and reheat. Serve with a garnish of finely chopped parsley.

LENTIL SOUP

250 g lentils, washed and soaked overnight, 1 small
onion, 1 small carrot, 1 small turnip, oil, 5 cups water
or stock, 1 dessertspoonful salt, 1 teaspoon pepper,
½ tablespoon flour, milk, 1 cup milk.

CHOP THE VEGETABLES into dice. Place the lentils and the vegetables in a saucepan with a little oil and stir until oil is absorbed. Do not allow to brown. Add 5 cups water or stock and seasoning. Boil until vegetables are soft, rub through a sieve, return to the saucepan, add ½ tablespoon flour mixed with a little milk and boil for a few minutes. Add 1 cup milk and reheat. Serve with croutons of toast.

SCOTCH BROTH

2 large onions, peeled and chopped, 30 g butter, 6 lamb
knuckles, 4 litres water, ¾ cup dried soup mix (split
peas, barley, lentils and noodles), 4 sticks celery,
chopped,
3 large carrots, peeled and diced, 1 parsnip, peeled and
diced, 1 small turnip, peeled and diced (optional),
2 teaspoons salt, black pepper, chopped parsley.

PLACE ONION AND BUTTER into a large saucepan or boiler. Fry
gently until soft, then add the remaining ingredients (except the
parsley) and simmer gently for 2 hours, stirring occasionally.
Serve with freshly ground black pepper and chopped parsley.

OXTAIL SOUP

1 oxtail, washed, 1 carrot, 1 turnip, 3 onions, 4 cloves,
1 dessertspoon salt, 5 cups water, flour.

CUT THE OXTAIL in pieces, brown in hot oil and drain. Put in a
pot with the carrot, turnip, onions, cloves, salt and water. Bring
to the boil and simmer for about 3 hours. Remove the tail, strain
the stock and thicken with flour. Some of the vegetables may be
added cut in small pieces just before serving. This is better
prepared a day in advance so that any fat is easier to remove.

TOMATO SOUP

1 kg tomatoes, sliced, or 1 × 1 kg tin of tomatoes,
1.25 litres stock, 1 small onion, chopped, ½ stick celery,
½ teaspoon salt, 60 g ham or bacon, parsley, thyme, bay
leaf, ½ teaspoon sugar, 30 g butter,
15 g sago (optional), pepper.

FRY THE TOMATOES and celery in oil for a few minutes but do not allow them to brown. Add the herbs, ham or bacon, seasonings and stock, and cook until the vegetables are tender. Blend or sieve the mixture, return to the saucepan and bring to the boil. Add the sago and cook until it is clear. Season to taste and serve.

PEA SOUP

500 g yellow split peas, 2 onions, peeled and sliced,
30 g butter, 500 g carrots, peeled and coarsely grated,
¼ bunch celery, chopped, 1 ham bone or a smoked hock
(or both), 4 litres water, thyme, salt and pepper,
fresh mint or parsley.

EMPTY SPLIT PEAS into a boiler. Sauté onions in butter until soft, then add to peas with carrots, celery and ham bone or hock. Pour in water and add thyme. Place lid on the boiler and simmer gently for about 2 hours, stirring occasionally. Remove bones, chop meat and return to the pot. Allow to heat through, taste and add freshly ground pepper and, if necessary, a little salt. Serve hot sprinkled with mint or parsley.

Salads, Vegetables and Vegetarian Dishes

HARICOT BEANS

250 g haricot beans, chopped parsley, butter, salt, pepper, lemon juice.

SOAK THE BEANS for 12 hours, place in a saucepan of cold water and let them come to the boil gradually. Simmer until tender. Drain and replace in the saucepan with butter, parsley, seasoning and a little lemon juice. Mix all ingredients well and reheat before serving.

CURRIED EGGS

4 hard-boiled eggs, ½ tablespoon oil, 1 small apple,
1 small onion, curry powder, salt, 1 teaspoon coconut,
3 teaspoons flour, 1 tablespoon chutney, 1½ cups milk
or stock.

CUT UP THE ONION and apple very finely and fry them until light brown in hot oil. Add the curry powder, salt, coconut, flour and chutney and fry until light brown. Add the milk or stock and stir over the heat until boiling. Simmer for ½ hour. Cut the hard-boiled eggs in half, add to the mixture and heat. Serve with rice.

EGGS À LA TRIPE

3 onions, 1 cup milk, little butter, 3 eggs, 1 tablespoon
flour, salt and pepper.

PEEL THE ONIONS and cut in quarters. Boil with salt in a cup of water. When soft drain off the water. Mix flour to a smooth paste with milk; add butter and pepper. Add this to the onions and allow to boil until it thickens, stirring constantly. Hard boil the eggs, shell and slice. Lift the onions with sauce into a hot dish and place eggs on top. Garnish with toast.

CELERY AND PEANUT SALAD

1 cup peanuts, 2 cups chopped celery, salt and pepper,
salad dressing, lettuce leaves.

SHELL AND SKIN THE PEANUTS, chop them and add them to the chopped celery. Season, mix in a little salad dressing and serve in lettuce cups.

ORANGE AND CELERY SALAD

2 oranges, lettuce leaves, 2 tablespoons celery, finely
chopped, celery curls, 2 tablespoons walnuts, finely
chopped, whole walnuts, vinegar and oil salad dressing.

ARRANGE SLICES of peeled orange on lettuce leaves. Sprinkle
finely chopped celery and walnuts on the centre of each slice of
orange. Chill thoroughly. Garnish with celery curls and walnuts.
Serve with dressing.

RAW VEGETABLE SALAD

1 young crisp cabbage, 1 carrot, 1 small onion,
250 g dates, 100 g sugar, 1 teaspoon salt, 1 sliced banana,
2 apples, 3 sticks celery, 1 tablespoon chopped nuts,
juice of 1 lemon, pepper.

WASH THE HEART of the cabbage and dry. Cut it up finely.
Scrape the carrot finely. Chop the onion finely. Peel and cut up
the apples. Put all these in a dish and sprinkle with sugar, lemon
juice, salt and a little pepper. Arrange the stoned dates and
chopped nuts on top, and serve with salad dressing.

*Mid pleasures and palaces
though we may roam,
Be it ever so humble
There's no place like home.*

Savoury Carrots

1 bunch carrots, butter, salt and pepper, 1 teaspoon
finely chopped parsley, 1 tablespoon finely chopped
onion, 1 cup stock.

WASH AND SCRAPE the carrots and cut them into rings about
5 mm thick. Put the butter in a saucepan and when it is melted
add the other ingredients. Toss over heat until the carrots are
covered with oil, then add the stock and simmer gently until
tender.

Stuffed Potatoes

4–5 potatoes, 3–4 tablespoons cooked meat, 1 teaspoon
chopped parsley, 2 tablespoons sauce *or* cream, *or* 1 egg,
seasoning.

CHOOSE POTATOES of equal size and good shape. Scrub well,
remove eyes and prick. Bake in a hot oven until soft — 45–60
minutes. Turn the potatoes occasionally so that they cook
evenly. Cut a piece from the top of each potato and scoop out
the centre without damaging the skin. Add this to the finely
chopped meat and parsley mixture. Season well and bind with
the sauce, cream or beaten egg. Refill the skins, piling high in the
centre, sprinkle breadcrumbs over the top and put a little butter
on each one. Heat in the oven and serve garnished with sprigs of
parsley.

Tomato Pie

BUTTER A PIE dish and fill up with alternate layers of sliced
tomatoes, sliced onions and breadcrumbs, with a little butter or
oil on top of the last layer. Bake at 200°C until browned. Serve
with roast beef or lamb.

VEGETABLE STEW

500 g lentils, 3 carrots, 3 turnips, 2 onions, 1 stalk celery,
3 potatoes, 1 cup milk, parsley, 1 tablespoon
tomato sauce, dry toast.

SOAK THE LENTILS overnight. Next day put them in cold water
with the carrots, turnips, onions, celery and potatoes, all peeled
and sliced. Let the mixture boil until tender, then add the milk,
the seasoning, a little parsley and tomato sauce. Serve hot with
plenty of dry toast.

VEGETABLE STOCK

1 cabbage, 2 carrots, 1 turnip, 3 large onions,
1 tablespoon butter, bouquet garni, 3–4 cloves, a few
peppercorns, 3.5 litres water, salt to taste.

WASH, SCRAPE AND PEEL all the vegetables. Cut them up very
small and place in a saucepan with the butter, bouquet garni and
seasoning. Let them fry gently or sweat in the butter for a few
minutes, stirring constantly to prevent burning. Pour in 3.5 litres
of cold water and salt to taste. When the water boils reduce heat
and simmer gently for 2–2½ hours. If necessary skim and strain
before use.

Fish

BAKED FLATHEAD

flathead (quantity depends on size of fish), stuffing, oil,
lemon slices, parsley, anchovy sauce or piquant sauce.

CLEAN, WASH AND DRY the fish. Press the stuffing lightly into the
opening made when cleaning the fish. Sew up the opening with
string or cotton. Brush over with oil, wrap in greaseproof paper
and bake in a moderate oven (180°C) for 15–20 minutes.
Remove the string or cotton, serve on a hot dish garnished with
lemon slices and parsley. The sauce should be served separately.

Stuffing

500 g raw white fish, without bone or skin,
½ tablespoon butter, ½ tablespoon flour,
½ cup fish stock or milk,
1–2 eggs, salt and pepper, grated lemon rind, lemon juice.

MELT THE BUTTER in a saucepan, stir in the flour, then the stock,
and beat the mixture over heat until it forms a stiff ball. Cool
this mixture, then beat into it the beaten eggs and seasoning.
Flake the fish, removing small bones. Beat the fish into the egg
mixture. Add grated lemon rind and lemon juice to taste.

BAKED BARRACOUTA

6 cutlets from a medium-sized barracouta, ½ tablespoon
plain flour, salt and pepper, juice of ½ lemon,
1 tablespoon butter, 1 tablespoon chopped parsley.

WASH AND DRY THE FISH and place the slices side by side in an
ovenproof dish. Mix the flour and seasonings together, and
sprinkle lemon juice over the fish. Mix the butter and parsley
and place in small pieces on the fish. Bake in a moderate oven
(200°C) for 20 minutes, basting occasionally. Serve on a hot dish
with the liquid strained over.

BAKED SCHNAPPER

2 schnapper, juice of 1 lemon, 2 tablespoons chopped
mushrooms, 2 teaspoons finely chopped parsley,
1 teaspoon finely chopped onion, salt and pepper,
1 tablespoon browned breadcrumbs,
½ tablespoon butter.

WASH, DRY AND FILLET the fish, place in a well-greased ovenproof
dish and sprinkle with the lemon juice. Mix the mushrooms,
parsley and onion together and season well. Spread this mixture
over the fish and cover thickly with the crumbs; dot with butter.
Bake in a fairly hot oven (220°C) for 15–20 minutes, depending
on the size of the fish. Serve in the same dish.

BAKED TRUMPETER

1 striped trumpeter, 1 tablespoon butter, 125 g bacon
rashers, 250 g tomatoes, ½ teaspoon mixed herbs, salt
and pepper, juice of 1 lemon, 2 tablespoons water or fish
stock, 1 tablespoon browned breadcrumbs.

WASH, CLEAN THE FISH and cut it into fillets. Butter a deep pie dish and put the fish in it. Place the bacon on top and then the peeled, sliced tomatoes sprinkled with herbs, salt and pepper. Add the lemon juice and water or stock. Melt the remainder of the butter, stir in the breadcrumbs and add the mixture to the pie dish. Bake for 30 minutes in a moderate oven (200°C). If cooked fish is used, cook for only 20 minutes.

BLACKFISH IN BATTER

1 blackfish, 2 tablespoons flour, salt and pepper,
½ tablespoon butter or oil, ½ cup tepid water, 1–2
eggs, oil for frying, parsley sprigs, wedges of lemon.

FILLET THE FISH; wash and wipe it, then cut each fillet in two. Sift the flour, salt and pepper into a basin and make a well in the centre. Add the butter or oil and stir in a little of the flour. Gradually add the water, beating in the flour. Fold in the stiffly whisked egg whites. Coat the fish in flour and dip each fillet into the batter. Fry in hot oil until golden brown. Serve garnished with fried parsley and lemon.

Eel with Lemon

eels, flour, vinegar or lemon juice, butter, salt and
pepper, grated lemon rind, white sauce, lemon juice.

SOAK THE EELS for several hours in cold salt water with a dash of
vinegar. Skin them and cut them into fillets. Dip the fillets in
flour, put them in a greased baking dish, sprinkle liberally with
vinegar or lemon juice, and add butter, salt and pepper. Add
grated lemon rind between the layers of fillets. Bake for 40
minutes in a moderate oven (200°C). Serve with a thin white
sauce, made with lemon juice and a little grated lemon rind.

Grilled Barracouta

2 very small barracouta, 1½ tablespoons butter, salt and
pepper, juice of ½ lemon, 1 tablespoon chopped parsley,
1 teaspoon anchovy essence.

CLEAN THE FISH, slit them open, wash and dry them, then brush them
over with melted butter. Season and place the fish under a heated grill.
Cook for 10 minutes, turning twice and brushing with melted butter
each time. Place on a heated serving dish. Mix the lemon juice, parsley
and anchovy essence into the remainder of the butter and pour this
sauce over the fish.

OYSTER FRITTERS

2 dozen oysters, 3 eggs, 1 cup milk, enough flour for a
stiff batter, seasoning, chopped parsley.

MAKE THE BATTER with the eggs, milk and some of the liquid
from the oysters. Chop the oysters and add them with salt,
pepper and parsley to the batter. Fry in hot oil, putting in about a
tablespoonful at a time.

POACHED MURRAY COD

1.5 kg Murray cod, salt, 1 lemon, 2 sprigs parsley.

WASH AND CLEAN THE FISH, scraping away any blood that gathers
inside near the backbone. Have ready a saucepan half full of
boiling water. Add enough salt, the juice of half the lemon and
parsley. Put the fish in and allow it to simmer gently (otherwise
the fish will break). Cook for 15 minutes, then test with a
skewer. Serve on a hot dish and garnish with slices of lemon.
Serve with parsley or egg sauce or plain melted butter.

SAND EELS

1 kg eels, skinned, 3 small onions, 6–8 mushrooms,
1 glass port wine, 1 tablespoon parsley, salt and pepper,
nutmeg, 1 teaspoon cornflour, 1 cup stock.

DIVIDE THE EELS into pieces. Cut up the onions. Peel and clean
the mushrooms. Fry the onions and mushrooms in butter and a
little flour. When nicely brown pour in the stock, then add the
port, parsley and seasoning; blend the cornflour and add it; then
add the pieces of eel. Stew very slowly until the eel is tender.

Meat and Game

MEAT PIE 1

1 ox kidney (optional), juice of ½ lemon, 3 bacon
rashers, 2 onions, 1.5–2 kg chuck steak, 2 cups water,
black pepper, salt, thyme, 1 stick celery, finely chopped,
3 tablespoons plain flour, shortcrust pastry, using
250 g flour.

SOAK THE KIDNEY in a little water with lemon juice for ½ hour
to remove any strong flavour. Fry chopped bacon in a large
heavy-based saucepan. When the fat starts to sizzle add the
sliced onion and fry until soft. Add chopped steak and finely
chopped kidney. Pour in water and season with pepper, salt and
thyme, then add the celery. Cover and simmer gently for about
1½ hours. Mix the flour with a little extra cold water, then stir
into the meat. Stir over the heat until thick. Pour into a deep pie
dish. Roll out the pastry, cut a few strips for a collar. Place these
on the wet rim of the pie dish and brush with milk or beaten egg.
Trim edges with a knife and press together with a fork to seal.
Make a few steam holes. Glaze with beaten egg or milk and bake
in a hot oven (230°C) for 30–40 minutes.

Be to my virtues very kind,
And to my faults a little blind.

A friendship such as thine and mine
No time or space can sever —
Our hearts that met in auld lang syne
Are linked in love forever.

MEAT PIE 2

500 g steak, 1 onion, 3 cloves, salt, sugar, flour,
short crust pastry.

DICE OR MINCE the steak. Roll the meat in flour, cut up the onion finely and put them both in a saucepan with enough water to cover well. Add the cloves, a pinch of sugar and salt. Simmer until cooked. Prepare a pie dish with short crust pastry and bake the pie at 230°C until it is nicely browned. Serve hot.

CAMP PIE

700 g shin of beef, 250 g bacon, 1 teaspoon salt, mace,
cayenne, ½ teaspoon mustard, 1 tablespoon gelatine,
1 beaten egg.

MINCE THE BEEF and bacon together. Add the salt, spices, mustard and gelatine to the meat. Bind the mixture with a beaten egg and pack it into a greased tin with a lid. Cover with buttered paper, press the mixture well down into the tin and put a lid on. Steam for 2½ hours, then remove the tin from the steamer and put a weight on the pie until it is firm. Turn it out on to a plate.

KEDGEREE

500 g cold cooked fish, 2 tablespoons rice, 2 hard-boiled
eggs, 1 tablespoon butter, salt and pepper, cayenne.

BOIL AND STRAIN THE RICE. Divide the fish into small flakes. Cut the egg whites into slices and sieve the yolks. Melt the butter in a saucepan; add to it the fish, rice, egg yolks and whites, salt, pepper and cayenne, and stir until hot. Turn the mixture into a hot dish and serve hot.

BEEF BRAISED IN BEER OR CIDER

700 g topside steak, flour, 4 carrots, sliced, 500 g onions,
sliced, 600–700 ml pale ale or cider, 1 tablespoon brown
sugar, salt and pepper, thyme, 1 bay leaf.

IN THE EVENING slice the topside about 1 cm thick, rub it in flour
and fry until brown on both sides with the carrots. Fry the
onions slowly until soft and coloured, then put alternate layers
of meat and onions in a casserole. Pour the ale or cider over the
meat and sprinkle with brown sugar. Season, add the herbs and
leave overnight. If necessary, add a little more ale or cider to
cover the meat and vegetables in the morning. Cook all day at
40–70°C or 3–4 hours at 120°C, closely covered.

ROAST CHICKEN

1 roasting chicken, salt and pepper, 2–3 rashers of bacon,
1 cup stock, oil for basting.

TRUSS THE CHICKEN, season lightly and cover with bacon. Roast
on a rack in the roasting dish in a fairly hot oven (180–200°C)
until tender — about 1–1½ hours. Baste frequently. Prick the
thigh to test for tenderness; if there is any trace of blood the
chicken is not cooked. The bacon may be removed 15–20
minutes before serving to allow the breast to brown. When the
chicken is cooked place on a hot meat dish, remove trussing
string and keep hot while making gravy.

Gravy

Pour excess fat and oil from roasting dish but keep the sediment.
Pour in stock and boil for 2–3 minutes. Season to taste and strain
into a hot sauceboat.

CASSEROLED CHICKEN AND MUTTON

1 boiling chicken, 1 lean shoulder of mutton,
500 g skinned tomatoes, 500 g onions, sliced, 250 g green
capsicums, 250 g marrow, peeled and cubed, 1 clove
garlic, crushed, salt and pepper, ½ bottle white wine or
cider, 200 g haricot beans or dried peas.

IN THE EVENING put the chicken into a large casserole dish with
the mutton, cut in 4 large pieces, around it. Add the tomatoes,
onions, capsicums, marrow, garlic, salt and pepper. Pour the
wine or cider over the meat and vegetables, and leave overnight.
Soak the beans or peas. Next morning drain the beans or peas
and add them to the casserole. Add water to cover. Cook all day
at 40–70°C. In the evening joint the chicken and remove its skin.
Serve with crusty bread.

CHICKEN PIE

1 cooked chicken, breadcrumbs, 1 onion, grated, salt and
pepper, 1 egg, separated, mashed potato.

REMOVE ALL THE FLESH from the bones of a cooked chicken, and
mince finely. Add an equal amount of breadcrumbs, a little
grated onion, salt and pepper; mix all together with the egg yolk.
Whip the egg white to a stiff froth and add it to the mixture.
Then put the mixture in a small pie dish and spread mashed
potato over the top. Bake in a moderate oven (200°C) until the
potato is brown and crisp. Serve hot with tomato sauce.

CORNISH PASTIES

500 g pastry, 250 g lean steak, 250 g potatoes, onions, salt
and pepper, 1 carrot or turnip, or both.

CUT UP THE MEAT and vegetables finely and sprinkle with a little
gravy or water. Roll out the pastry. Cut it into round pieces
about 15 cm in diameter. Put the meat and vegetables in the
centre; fold over and press the edges into a frill. Bake for ½ hour
at 230°C.

RABBIT PIE

1 rabbit, milk, salt and pepper, flour, bacon, sliced,
veal stuffing.

CUT THE RABBIT into joints and put them into a pie dish. Cover
with milk and cook in the oven for about 2 hours at 200°C. Take
out and add salt and pepper and thicken with flour. Lay a few
slices of bacon on the top. Cover with 2 cm or so of veal stuffing
and bake for another hour at 180°C.

RABBIT STEW

2 young rabbits, white wine vinegar, 1 litre milk,
1 handful barley, 1 carton real cream, 1 bunch leeks,
1 bouquet garni, salt and black pepper, carrots, celery,
new potatoes.

JOINT THE RABBIT and soak the pieces in cold salted water with a
dash of white wine vinegar for about 1 hour. Rinse and place in
a saucepan, cover with fresh cold water and boil for about 3
minutes to blanch the meat. Rinse off any scum and place the
meat in a casserole dish. Cover with milk and finely sliced leeks.
Add bouquet garni and barley, and cook slowly for about 1 hour
before testing. Add par-cooked carrots, whole new potatoes and
chunks of celery. Cook for about 10 minutes, season with salt
and black pepper, stir in the cream (do not allow to boil), garnish
with finely chopped parsley and serve.

CURRIED RABBIT

2 onions, 1 tablespoon oil, 1 apple, curry powder, 2 cups
water, salt, 1 tablespoon stoned raisins, 1 rabbit,
1 tablespoon flour, juice of ½ lemon.

SLICE THE ONIONS and fry until brown in hot oil. Peel, core and
grate the apple and add to the onion. Mix curry powder with
water and a pinch of salt; add to and boil with the onion and
apple. Chop the raisins and, when the curry is boiling, add the
rabbit cut into neat joints. Simmer gently for 2 hours; 10 minutes
before serving, add flour and the strained lemon juice.

RABBIT CROQUETTES

1 rabbit, cooked, an equal quantity of ham or bacon,
grated lemon peel, chopped parsley, salt, cayenne,
1 tablespoon flour, 2 eggs, breadcrumbs.

FINELY MINCE all the meat from the rabbit, add the bacon or ham,
also minced, season with the lemon peel, parsley and cayenne.
Place in a mixing bowl. Add flour and 1 egg. Mix well, then
form the mixture into rolls, dip in beaten egg, then in breadcrumbs, and fry in hot oil. Serve garnished with fried parsley.

INDIAN DEVIL

1 tablespoon chutney, 1 tablespoon tomato sauce,
1 tablespoon cold gravy, 1 tablespoon butter,
1½ teaspoons salt, pepper or mustard, cold cooked meat.

MIX ALL INGREDIENTS together well and add thin slices of cooked meat. Stir gently until heated and serve.

ROASTING BEEF, VEAL, LAMB AND PORK

PREHEAT THE OVEN. Wipe the joint and tie in shape. Stand the joint on a wire rack or grid in the baking dish. Put oil (about 2 tablespoons) on the joint and place it in a hot oven (230°C) for 5 minutes, then lessen the heat until the joint is cooked. For red meats allow 20 minutes for every 500 g of meat and an additional 25 minutes. For white meats allow 25 minutes for every 500 g of meat and an additional 25 minutes. For any joint weighing less than 1 kg allow about 1 hour for cooking. Baste meat as often as convenient while cooking and turn it at least once. Bake vegetables such as potato, pumpkin, marrow and parsnips in the same dish and serve with gravy. Add the vegetables 1 hour before serving.

Gravy

2 level dessertspoons flour, 1 dessertspoon oil and
dripping from roasting dish, 1 cup stock or water,
salt and pepper.

REMOVE MEAT and rack from roasting dish. Pour off oil into basin, leaving about 1 dessertspoon in dish. Add flour to pan and brown over heat, stirring to a smooth paste. Add stock or water and stir until boiling. Season and serve.

PIGEON PIE

2 pigeons, 250 g rump steak, 125 g ham or bacon, 2 cups
stock, 2 hard-boiled eggs, salt and pepper, puff pastry,
using 500 g flour, egg or milk to glaze.

REMOVE THE FEET from the pigeons and split each bird in half.
Cut the steak into thin slices, cut the bacon into strips and slice
the eggs. Put all ingredients in layers in a pie dish, seasoning the
layers well, and seasoning each half bird. Three-quarters fill the
dish. Cover with puff pastry, glaze and cook in a hot oven
(220°C) until pastry is risen and set, then lower heat to 180°C
and bake for 1 hour more. Cut the toes off the pigeon's feet and
scald the feet. Before serving the pie, fill it with the remainder of
the hot seasoned stock and fix the feet in an upright position in a
hole previously made in the pastry.

HAM AND EGG PIE

125 g mushrooms, 4 tablespoons milk, salt and pepper,
200 g cooked ham, 100 g cooked peas, 2 hard-boiled eggs,
1 teaspoon mixed mustard, flaky pastry using 250 g flour,
egg or milk.

PREPARE THE MUSHROOMS and simmer for 10 minutes in milk
seasoned with salt and pepper. Chop the ham roughly and mix
with the peas, hard-boiled eggs, mushrooms, mustard and
seasoning. Divide the pastry into 2 unequal portions. Roll out
the larger piece, cover an ovenproof dish or plate and trim the
edges. Put in the prepared filling. Roll out the remaining pastry
and cover the pie. Flake and scallop the edges and decorate as
desired. Glaze the top with beaten egg or milk. Bake for 45
minutes, first in a very hot oven (230–250°C) until set and then
at 180°C until well risen and firm.

The seasons come and the seasons go,
The summer sun and the winter snow,
The springtime flowers and the autumn gold,
But the sun's still shining like a ball of gold.

OXTAIL STEW

2 oxtails, 3 large onions, 4 carrots, 2 garlic cloves,
1 tablespoon tomato paste, 1 teaspoon sugar, 4 bay
leaves, thyme, ½ bottle red wine, beef stock, plain flour,
oil, black pepper, parsley.

JOINT THE OXTAILS and trim off the fat. Roll the pieces in lightly seasoned flour and brown a few pieces at a time in hot oil. Remove to a casserole dish. Brown the chopped onions in the same pan, adding more oil if necessary. As they brown add a little water and turn constantly to stop sticking or burning. When golden brown pour over the oxtail pieces. Cut the carrots into rounds, flour them lightly and fry briefly in the same pan. Pour the red wine into the pan and stir in the tomato paste, crushed garlic, sugar, bay leaves and fresh thyme. Pour over the oxtail. Add a little beef stock to cover the pieces and cook in a low oven (150°C) for 3 hours. During cooking check the liquid, adding more if necessary, and turn the pieces. Leave until next day. Carefully remove fat and taste for seasoning. Add salt if necessary and fresh black pepper before reheating gently.

CURRIED KIDNEYS

4–5 sheep's kidneys, ½ tablespoon butter, 1
dessertspoon rice flour, curry powder, 1 onion, 1 small
apple, 1 cup stock, chutney, salt and pepper, lemon juice.

SKIN AND SPLIT the kidneys and remove the fat. Heat butter and brown kidneys; lift out into a saucepan. Slice onion thinly and chop apple and brown in butter. Add flour, curry powder, chutney, salt, pepper and lemon juice. Stir well and pour in the stock gradually. Boil 3 minutes; pour over kidneys and simmer for 45–60 minutes. Serve on a hot dish with boiled rice.

Roast Quail

quails, fat bacon, rounds of toast, watercress, lemon.

TRUSS THE QUAILS. Cover with fat bacon and roast for 15–20 minutes, basting frequently. Serve very hot on rounds of toast, garnished with watercress and lemon.

Shepherd's Pie

any cooked meat, 1 small onion, finely chopped,
1 dessertspoon flour, ½ cup stock or gravy, mashed
potatoes, 1 dessertspoon tomato sauce, pepper, salt,
1 dessertspoon butter.

REMOVE SKIN, gristle and some fat from the meat; mince or chop finely. Put in a saucepan with gravy, flour and flavourings, and cook slowly for 5 minutes. Put into a greased pie dish and cover with mashed potato. Spread butter on top. Place in a hot oven (230°C) until browned.

Optional: Instead of gravy or stock, heat a little oil in a frying pan, slice 1 small onion thinly and fry until brown. Add 15 g flour and brown well. Stir in gradually 1 cup of water. Boil for 3 minutes. Season and strain.

Carpet-bag Steak

1 kg piece of topside, pocketed for stuffing.

Stuffing
1 tablespoon butter, 12–18 oysters, 125 g mushrooms,
3 tablespoons breadcrumbs, 1 tablespoon chopped
parsley, grated rind of ½ lemon, salt and paprika, 1 egg.

HEAT THE BUTTER and toss the oysters and roughly chopped mushrooms into it; cook for 5 minutes. Transfer the mixture to a basin and mix in the breadcrumbs, parsley, lemon rind and seasoning. Stir in the beaten egg. Press the mixture into the pocket in the steak and sew or skewer the edges together. Roast in a warm oven (180°C) for 2 hours to prevent shrinkage. Serve with roast potatoes and pumpkin.

PIG AND RABBIT BRAWN

½ pig's head, 1 rabbit, 2 onions, chopped, 1 carrot, chopped, 2 bay leaves, 2 cloves, salt and pepper, cayenne, mace.

SOAK THE PIG'S HEAD and the rabbit, then simmer both until tender. Remove the meat from the bones and cut it into small cubes. Return the bones to the liquid with the onions, carrots, cloves, bay leaves and seasoning. Reduce the stock slowly to 1 cup, strain it and add the mace. Add the stock to the meat, place the mixture in a wet mould and allow it to set, pressing down with a weight on top.

LAMB'S FRY AND BACON

liver, bacon, seasoned flour, chopped parsley.

WASH AND DRY the liver and cut it into thin slices. Dip each slice in the seasoned flour. Fry slices of bacon until the fat is transparent, then remove them from the pan and keep them hot. Fry the liver for about 8–10 minutes, turning frequently. Remove from the pan and drain off most of the remaining bacon fat. Sprinkle in a little more seasoned flour and stir until well browned. Add a cup of water and stir until boiling. Strain the gravy if necessary, return it to the pan, add the liver and bacon, and simmer gently until all are well heated through. Serve with chopped parsley.

SPICED MUTTON

500 g leg chops, 2 tablespoons chopped celery,
30 g dripping, 1 teaspoon chutney, ginger, salt, 1 cup
stock or water, 2 tablespoons chopped onions, curry
powder, allspice, ½ tablespoon ground rice, cloves,
1 tablespoon sultanas.

CUT MEAT into neat pieces and sprinkle with spices. Brown meat and onions in oil. Add the ground rice and stir well. Add the liquid and celery. Simmer slowly until tender — about 1½ hours. Half an hour before serving, add the sultanas; 5 minutes before serving, add the chutney.

SQUAB PIE

1 kg chops (pork or lamb), 1 kg sour apples, sugar,
allspice, salt and pepper, 1 onion, finely chopped, 1 cup
gravy, pastry.

CUT AWAY ALL THE FAT from the chops, and chop off the long bones. Peel, core and slice the apples, and place a layer of them in the bottom of a pie dish, with a little sugar and allspice. Next add a layer of chops seasoned with salt and pepper and some finely chopped onion. Continue until the dish is full, pour in some gravy and cover with pastry. Bake in a moderate oven for 1½ hours.

STEAK AND MUSHROOM PIE

700 g blade or round steak, 1 rasher bacon, flour,
1 onion, finely chopped, salt and pepper, about
20 mushrooms, butter, puff pastry, yolk of 1 egg.

CUT UP THE MEAT and bacon, coat with flour and place in a greased pie dish with the onion, salt and pepper. Cover the dish and place it in a moderate oven (200°C) for 1½ hours. Allow to cool. Fry the mushrooms in butter and add them to the pie. Season with salt and pepper. Wet the edges of the dish and cover with puff pastry. Brush the top with egg yolk and bake for about 30 minutes until golden brown.

TOAD IN THE HOLE

500 g beef or pork sausages, oil

Batter
4 tablespoons plain flour, salt, 1 egg, 1 cup milk.

PREHEAT THE OVEN to 200°C. Place the sausages in a medium-sized roasting tin with a little oil. Set aside. Sift the flour and salt into a mixing bowl and make a well in the centre. Break the egg into it and add about ⅓ of the milk. Mix gently. Add remaining milk gradually, stirring all the time. Beat well for 1 minute. Place the sausages in the oven for 10 minutes. Remove from the oven and pour the batter into the dish. Replace the tin near the top of the oven and bake for 25–30 minutes or until the batter is well risen and crisp. Serve at once, cut in pieces.

COOLGARDIE STEW

750 g topside steak, 2 hard-boiled eggs, 1 onion, 1 heaped tablespoon flour, salt, cayenne pepper or curry powder, 1 egg, 250 g bacon rashers, flour, 500 g tomatoes, juice of 1 lemon, 2½ cups stock or water.

CUT THE STEAK into thin 12 cm lengths. Chop the hard-boiled eggs and onion, and mix them with the tablespoon of flour, the seasonings and beaten egg. Remove the bacon rind and cut the bacon into 8 cm lengths. Roll a teaspoonful of egg mixture in each strip of bacon, and then in one of the pieces of steak. Secure with a toothpick. Toss in flour and sear in hot oil. Transfer from pan to casserole, add the tomatoes, skinned and sliced, lemon juice and stock or water. Place in a moderate oven (200°C) and allow to cook for 2 hours. Remove the toothpicks.

VEAL AND HAM PIE

1 kg neck or breast of veal, salt and pepper, 750 g ham or
bacon, 2 hard-boiled eggs, balls of stuffing, puff or rough
puff pastry, mace, 1 lemon, gravy.

CUT THE VEAL into small squares and put into an ovenproof dish
or saucepan, season with salt and pepper, cover with cold water
and cook gently either in the oven or on the stove for 2 hours.
Meanwhile cut the ham into narrow strips and the eggs into thin
slices. Make the balls of stuffing and fry them lightly in a little
hot oil. Roll out the pastry and cut a piece to cover the top of the
pie dish. Line the edge of the dish with the pastry trimmings.
Allow the meat to cool slightly, then cover the bottom of the pie
dish with meat, add a few strips of ham and slices of egg.
Sprinkle lightly with salt, pepper, mace and grated lemon rind,
then intersperse with the stuffing balls. Repeat until the dish is
full, then half fill the dish with gravy. Put on the pastry cover,
moisten and press the edges together. Make a hole in the centre
of the top, decorate with pastry leaves, brush over with egg and
bake for 45–60 minutes in a fairly hot oven (220°C). As soon as
the pie is baked pour a little more well-seasoned gravy through
the hole in the top and, when served hot, serve with gravy made
from the liquid in which the meat was stewed.

Cakes, Biscuits and Puddings

AUSTRALIAN CAKE

Pastry
90 g butter, 185 g plain flour, salt, 2–3 tablespoons
water.

Filling
2 tablespoons raspberry jam, 4 tablespoons currants.

Sponge
90 g butter, 90 g castor sugar, vanilla essence, 2 eggs
(room temperature), 150 g SR flour, salt,
2 tablespoons milk.

MAKE THE PASTRY by rubbing the butter into the sifted flour and
salt, then mixing to a dough with water. Knead on a lightly
floured board, then roll out to line the bottom of a 20 cm cake
tin. Spread with the jam, then sprinkle the currants on top.
Cream the butter and sugar for the sponge; add the vanilla. Add
the eggs gradually and beat well. Fold in the sifted flour and salt
alternately with the milk. Spread this mixture on top of the
currants and bake for 40–45 minutes in a moderate oven
(180°C).

AFTERNOON TEA CAKE

125 g chocolate, 100 g butter, 125 g castor sugar, 3 eggs, separated, 100 g SR flour, almond essence.

GRATE THE CHOCOLATE and melt it slowly, either in a jar in the oven or over boiling water on the stove. Cream the butter and sugar, then add the egg yolks and chocolate, and beat for a few minutes. Whip the egg whites to a stiff froth, and sift the flour. Add a little flour and a little egg white alternately to the other mixture until all is blended lightly together. Half fill small prepared tins with the mixture and bake in a moderate oven (200°C) for about 15 minutes.

APRICOTS AND RICE

60 g rice, 2 lemons, 600 ml milk, 185 g sugar, 2 eggs, 12 fresh apricots, 1 tablespoon apricot jam.

SIMMER THE RICE, the rind of 1 lemon cut into strips and the milk in a double boiler until the rice is tender. Take out the lemon rind, stir in ⅓ of the sugar beaten with the eggs; cook without boiling. Place a jar in the centre of a glass serving dish and pile the rice around it, sloping it towards the edge of the dish. Leave to become cold. Strain the lemon juice over the remainder of the sugar, place over a low heat to dissolve the sugar, then bring the syrup to the boil. Add the washed, halved and stoned apricots and a few kernels blanched and shredded. Cook gently until tender but not broken. Remove the jar and place the apricots in the space it occupied, piling them high up in the centre. Add the apricot jam to the syrup and strain it over the apricots. Serve when quite cold.

APRICOT MOULD

24 fresh apricots, 125 g sugar, 300 ml lemon jelly,
1 dessertspoon powdered gelatine, 300 ml custard,
60 g castor sugar, juice of 1 lemon.

HALVE THE APRICOTS and remove the stones. Dissolve the sugar in 150 ml water, then bring to the boil. Put the apricot halves into the same pan and remove 6 pieces when they are just cooked. When the remainder are soft sieve or blend them. Line a mould with jelly and decorate it with the 6 pieces of cooked apricot. Soak the gelatine in 3 tablespoons of cold water for 10 minutes, then dissolve it by stirring over boiling water. Mix the apricot pulp and custard together, add the sugar and lemon juice and dissolved gelatine. Mix quickly and thoroughly, turn into the prepared mould and chill until set. Turn out on to a glass dish.

AUNT KITTY'S CAKE

100 g butter, 100 g sugar, vanilla essence, 2 eggs,
1 tablespoon sultanas, ½ tablespoon cut peel,
150 g SR flour, 30 g plain flour, 1 teaspoon mixed spice,
3 tablespoons milk.

Filling
2 oranges, 1 lemon, 150 ml water, 60 g sugar,
2 tablespoons cornflour.

CREAM THE BUTTER and sugar and add a few drops of vanilla. Add the eggs gradually and beat well. Stir in the sultanas and peel, then fold in the sifted flours and spice alternately with the milk. Transfer into two 18 cm sandwich tins. Bake in a moderate oven (180°C) for about 15 minutes. Allow the cakes to cool.

Finely grate the rind of 1 orange and the lemon; squeeze all the fruit and strain the juice. Blend the cornflour and sugar with some of the water; put the rest on to heat with the fruit juices and grated rinds. Bring almost to the boil, pour over the blended cornflour, return to the pan and stir until boiling. Cook for 2 minutes, then allow to cool. Sandwich the cakes together with the filling. Sprinkle with icing sugar or ice with orange or lemon glacé icing and decorate.

APPLE SNOW

6 Granny Smith apples, 2 cloves, ½ cup water,
2 egg whites, ¼ cup sugar.

PEEL, QUARTER and core the apples, then place them in a saucepan with the cloves and water. Cover and simmer gently until the apples are fluffy, then tip them into a colander to drain and cool (the apples should be fairly dry). Remove cloves. Whip the egg whites until stiff and white, then gradually whip in the sugar. Add the apples, then beat until they are white and frothy. Transfer to a serving dish.

APPLE PEARL CAKES

60 g butter, 100 g castor sugar, lemon essence, 1 egg,
1 heaped tablespoon grated apple, 185 g SR flour, pinch
of salt, 5 tablespoons milk.

CREAM THE BUTTER and sugar with a few drops of lemon essence added. Add the egg gradually and beat in well. Stir in the apple, then fold in the sifted flour and salt alternately with the milk. Place dessertspoonsful of the mixture into patty cases and bake in a fairly hot oven (220°C) for 12–15 minutes. When cold, ice with lemon or orange glacé icing.

BREAD AND BUTTER CUSTARD

2 slices bread, butter, ½ tablespoon sugar, nutmeg, salt,
2 eggs, 1 cup milk, ½ tablespoon sultanas,
¼ tablespoon lemon peel.

BUTTER AND CUT up the bread into squares. Remove the crusts. Place it in a pie dish with the sultanas and peel. Beat the eggs, sugar and salt together and mix with the milk. Pour the mixture over the bread. Sprinkle nutmeg over the top and add the remaining butter in tiny lumps. Stand the pie dish in a dish or tray of water and bake at 150–160°C until set and brown.

BASIC BISCUITS

185 g SR flour, ½ teaspoon salt, 125 g butter,
125 g castor sugar, 1 egg, vanilla essence, 2 tablespoons
finely chopped walnuts.

SIFT THE FLOUR and salt and set aside. Cream the butter and sugar. Beat the egg and a few drops of vanilla together. Gradually mix in with the butter and sugar. Stir in the dry ingredients and chopped nuts and mix thoroughly. Turn out the dough on to a lightly floured surface and shape it into a fat roll. Cut off slices about 5 mm thick, place on a lightly greased tray and bake in the centre of a moderate oven (180°C) for 15 minutes. If the roll of dough is wrapped tightly in foil, it may be refrigerated until required; you simply slice off as many biscuits as you wish and return the remaining dough to the refrigerator.

CARAMEL SELF-SAUCING PUDDING

60 g butter, ⅓ cup sugar, 1 egg, ½ cup milk, grated rind
of 1 lemon, 1½ cups SR flour, 1 cup sultanas.

Caramel Sauce

¾ cup brown sugar, 1 tablespoon golden syrup, 1 cup
water, 60 g butter, juice of ½ lemon.

PUT BUTTER, sugar, egg, milk, lemon rind and flour into a basin. Beat with a wooden spoon for a minute or so. Mix in sultanas, then put the mixture into a greased casserole dish. Put sugar, golden syrup, water and butter into a saucepan and stir over a medium heat to dissolve the sugar, then boil for 2–3 minutes. Add lemon juice, then pour syrup over the cake mixture. Bake in a moderate oven (200°C) for 1 hour. Serve hot or cold.

CARROT PUDDING

250 g young carrots, pinch of salt, 185 g butter,
125 g castor sugar, 2 egg whites, 250 g breadcrumbs,
125 g glacé cherries, 1 teaspoon ground cinnamon,
a little milk.

GREASE A 1.25 litre basin. Simmer the peeled and chopped carrots until tender. Strain and sieve. Cream the butter and sugar. Add the carrot pulp, breadcrumbs, cherries (quartered) and cinnamon. Add enough milk, if necessary, to achieve a stiff, dropping consistency. Whisk the egg whites stiffly and fold them into the mixture. Pour into a well-greased basin and cover. Steam for 2¼–2½ hours.

CHOCOLATE APPLE CAKE

500 g cooking apples, 1 teaspoon bicarbonate of soda,
2 cups SR flour, 2 tablespoons cocoa, 125 g margarine or
butter, 250 g sugar, ½ teaspoon vanilla.

PEEL AND CORE the apples; slice them thickly. Put in a saucepan with very little water. Cover the pan and cook gently until soft, mashing them occasionally to hasten cooking. Meanwhile sift the flour and cocoa together thoroughly and return to the sieve. Have the soda ready measured out, and grease a large, deep square cake tin. Cream the margarine with the sugar and vanilla. When the apples are cooked, remove from the heat and stir in the soda at once. While the mixture is still fizzing, turn it into the creamed butter and sugar and beat thoroughly. Sift in about half the flour and cocoa mixture. Stir and beat quickly. Stir in the remainder and beat quickly again. Turn at once into the prepared tin and bake in a moderate oven (200°C) for 30–45 minutes. *Note:* It is important that the apples are well strained; too much moisture will spoil the cake.

CHOCOLATE FUDGE CAKE

100 g butter, 1 cup sugar, 1 egg, 2 tablespoons cocoa,
pinch of bicarbonate of soda, ½ cup milk, 1½ cups
plain flour, 2 teaspoons baking powder, pinch of salt,
½ cup boiling water, vanilla, melted chocolate.

CREAM THE BUTTER and sugar. Add the egg, cocoa and a pinch of bicarbonate of soda dissolved in the milk. Sift the flour and add it to the mixture with the baking powder and salt. Then add the boiling water and a little vanilla. Bake in a moderate oven until the cake leaves the sides of the tin. Ice with melted chocolate.

CHOCOLATE JELLY

4 tablespoons grated chocolate, ½ cup sugar, 1 teaspoon
vanilla essence, 30 g gelatine, 600 ml whipped cream.

BOIL THE GRATED CHOCOLATE in a cup of water; add the sugar and the vanilla. Soak the gelatine in cold water for half an hour; add it to the chocolate and boil a few minutes. Remove from the heat and allow to cool. When cold mix in the cream. Pour into a mould and chill until firm.

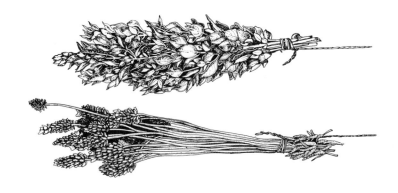

CONVENT CREAM

15 g gelatine, 300 ml cold water, ½ cup castor sugar,
250 ml boiling water, juice of 2 lemons, 4 egg whites.

Custard

500 ml milk, 4 egg yolks.

DISSOLVE THE GELATINE in hot water. Add sugar, lemon juice and cold water. Stir well until sugar dissolves. Add the egg whites. Pour the mixture into a glass dish and leave to stand until set. Make the custard and pour over.

CRUMPETS

2 eggs, 2 teaspoons sugar, 250 g flour, milk.

BREAK THE EGGS into a basin. Beat slightly and add the sugar. Sift the flour in another basin and pour in the eggs; mix to make a light dough. (A little milk may be needed.) Working quickly, roll out 1 cm thick and cut into rounds. Prick with a fork. Bake in a hot oven (250°C) for 10 minutes. Tear open and butter while hot. Serve at once.

DATE PUDDING

250 g SR flour, salt, 100 g butter, 100 g castor sugar,
200 g chopped stoned dates, 1 egg, milk.

GREASE A BASIN. Sift together the flour and salt. Rub the butter into the flour. Add the sugar and dates and mix well together. Mix to a soft dropping consistency with the egg and milk. Put the mixture into the basin. Cover with greased paper and steam for 1½ hours until firm in the centre.

Friendship, like gold,
needs the acid test of adversity
to determine its value.

DOUGHNUTS

250 g SR flour, 1 tablespoon butter, 1 egg, milk, jam, salt.

SIFT THE FLOUR and salt into a basin, rub in the butter and add the sugar. Make a soft dough with egg and milk. Knead lightly, and roll out 5 mm thick. Cut out with a round cutter. Put a teaspoon of jam in the middle of half the pieces; brush over the others with beaten egg. Place the two halves together and press the edges firmly. Fry in a saucepan of hot oil, 3–4 at a time. Drain and roll in icing sugar. Eat when freshly cooked.

EGGLESS FRUIT CAKE

250 g butter, 250 g brown sugar, 250 g currants, 250 g sultanas, 3 tablespoons raisins, $\frac{1}{2}$ tablespoon shelled almonds, blanched, $\frac{1}{2}$ tablespoon shelled walnuts, 450 ml warm water, 450 g SR flour, 1 teaspoon salt, 1 teaspoon mixed spice, nutmeg.

PUT THE BUTTER, sugar, fruit, nuts and water into a saucepan and bring gradually to the boil, stirring all the time. Boil gently for 5 minutes. Allow to become quite cold. Sift flour with salt, spice and nutmeg, and stir into the cold mixture. Turn into a prepared cake tin and bake in a moderate oven (180°C) for 2–2$\frac{1}{2}$ hours.

FREE KIRK PUDDING

2 tablespoons currants, 2 tablespoons raisins, 2 tablespoons sugar, 3 tablespoons suet, 3 tablespoons SR flour, $\frac{1}{2}$ teaspoon mixed spice, salt, lemon peel, 1 egg, milk.

MIX ALL INGREDIENTS together with a little milk. Steam for 3 hours.

GINGERNUTS

4 tablespoons SR flour, salt, 1 teaspoon ground ginger,
1 teaspoon mixed spice, 1 tablespoon butter,
1 tablespoon golden syrup.

SIFT THE FLOUR, spices and salt. Add the butter and rub in. Stir in the sugar. Warm the syrup over a low heat until it is runnier but not very hot. Pour it into the flour mixture and mix to a soft dough. Roll into small balls. Place the balls well apart on the baking tray and flatten each one. Bake at 180°C for 15 minutes in the centre of the oven.

GLAZED FRUIT SALAD CAKE

90 g butter, 125 g sugar, grated lemon rind, 2 eggs,
vanilla essence, 185 g SR flour, ½ cup milk, 2 bananas,
sliced pineapple, drained cherries, cream.

Glazing
1 dessertspoon gelatine, 1 cup water, ¼ cup lemon juice,
60 g sugar.

THOROUGHLY GREASE a recessed tin. Cream the butter and sugar and add the grated lemon rind. Add the eggs one at a time and beat well, then add vanilla essence. Sift the flour 3 times and add to the mixture alternately with the milk. Place the mixture in the tin and bake in a moderate oven (180°C) for 30–40 minutes. Turn out and cool. Arrange sliced bananas, pineapple and cherries in the recess in the cake. Make glazing by dissolving the gelatine in water, adding lemon juice and sugar, and heating slowly, stirring constantly. Cover the cake with cooled glazing and decorate the edge with cream.

GOLDEN SYRUP PUDDING

3 tablespoons golden syrup, 125 g butter, ½ cup castor sugar, 1 teaspoon vanilla essence, 2 eggs, 1½ cups SR flour, ½ cup milk.

GREASE A SMALL pudding basin well with butter. Pour golden syrup in the bottom. Cream butter, sugar and vanilla essence. Beat in the eggs one at a time, fold in sifted flour, then stir in milk. Add the pudding mixture to the basin on top of the golden syrup. Cover the basin or put its lid on and put it into boiling water. Cover the pot and simmer gently for 1½ hours. Allow to stand for a few minutes before turning out.

HURRY-SCURRY CAKE

1 cup SR flour, 1 cup sugar, ½ cup milk, 2 teaspoons marmalade, 1 egg.

STIR THE MARMALADE, the milk and the well-beaten egg into the flour and sugar. Grease a baking dish, put the mixture into it, flatten the top and brush with a little milk and sugar. Bake in a hot oven (220°C) for about 20–25 minutes.

LAMINGTONS

250 g butter, 250 g sugar, 3 eggs, 375 g SR flour, salt,
185 ml milk, vanilla essence, warm chocolate icing,
dessicated coconut.

LINE A 20 cm square cake tin with greaseproof paper. Cream
butter and sugar; add well-beaten eggs. Add flour and salt sifted
together. Lastly, fold in milk and vanilla essence. Place in the tin
and bake in a moderate oven (180°C) for 30–40 minutes. When
cold, cut into 4 cm squares. Dip each square into thin warm
chocolate icing and allow to drain a little. Roll in coconut and
allow to set.

LEMON CHIFFON PIE

2 egg yolks, 120 g sugar, salt, rind of ½ lemon,
1 dessertspoon gelatine, juice of 1 lemon,
3 tablespoons water, 2 egg whites.

BEAT THE EGG YOLKS with half the sugar, add a pinch of salt,
lemon juice and rind and half the water. Cook over hot water
until mixture thickens. Add gelatine soaked in remaining hot
water and stir until dissolved. Cool. When the mixture begins to
set, fold in the egg whites stiffly beaten with the remaining
sugar. Pour into tart plate lined with biscuit crumb crust or into
a cooked pastry shell. Chill before serving.

LEMON DELICIOUS PUDDING

30 g butter, 60 g castor sugar, 30 g flour, 2 lemons or
oranges, 2 eggs, separated, 1 cup milk.

CREAM THE BUTTER and sugar, add the sifted flour, grated rind and juice of the fruit, egg yolks and milk. Lastly fold in the stiffly whisked egg whites. Transfer the mixture to a greased pie dish, stand in a baking dish of water and bake in a cool oven (150°C) for 45 minutes. Serve with unwhipped cream.

LEMON SNOW

600 ml milk, 4 tablespoons cornflour, 4 tablespoons sugar, 2 lemons, 2 egg whites.

BLEND CORNFLOUR with some of the milk and put the remainder on to heat. Add the cornflour to the milk gradually, bring to the boil and cook for 3 minutes, stirring constantly. Add sugar and stir until dissolved. Add strained lemon juice and allow to cool. Beat egg whites stiffly and fold into the mixture. Pour into a wet mould to set. Decorate the mould with slices of lemon if desired. Serve with custard sauce.

LOQUAT PIE OR TART

1 kg loquats, 100 g sugar, 150 ml water, 1 tablespoon
lemon juice, short crust pastry using 200 g flour.

WASH THE FRUIT, cut them in half and remove the stones. Make
a syrup with the sugar, water and lemon juice. Add the loquat
stones and simmer for 10 minutes, then strain. Return the liquid
to the saucepan, add the fruit and cook until it is tender.
Transfer to a pie dish and allow the mixture to cool before
covering the top with pastry. Cut a hole in the top, brush with
glaze and bake for 20 minutes in a moderate oven (180°C). Serve
either hot or cold.

MADEIRA CAKE

300 g SR flour, salt, 500 g butter, 500 g sugar, 4 eggs,
200 ml milk, essence, 15 g carraway seeds (optional),
icing sugar.

PREPARE THE OVEN and tin. Sift the dry ingredients. Cream the
butter and sugar. Add the eggs one at a time, beating each one
well. Fold in the flour and add the essence and milk gradually
during the folding. Place the mixture in a cake tin and sift a small
quantity of icing sugar on top. Bake in a moderate oven (200°C)
for 1½ hours.

OLD MAID'S PUDDING

60 g breadcrumbs, 60 g SR flour, 60 g grated apple,
60 g minced suet, 1 tablespoon currants, 1 tablespoon
chopped candied peel, 1 egg, a little milk.

RUB ALL THE dry ingredients together, then mix with the egg and
milk. Press into a well-greased basin and boil or steam for 1–1½
hours.

Australian Household Companion

MELBOURNE PANCAKES

125 g SR flour, salt, 1 egg yolk, 150 ml sour milk,
1 dessertspoon butter, melted, 1 dessertspoon hot water,
oil, 1 cup ripe fruit, mashed and sweetened,
15 g castor sugar.

SIFT THE FLOUR and salt into a bowl. Add the egg yolk and beat in with some of the flour. Add the milk gradually and beat to a smooth batter. Cover and allow to stand for ½ hour. Add the butter and the hot water. Heat a small amount of oil in a pan and cook the pancakes in the usual way. For each person sandwich 3 pancakes with a layer of fruit in between. Sprinkle with castor sugar and serve.

MOUNT LOFTY PUDDING

1 cup SR flour, 2 tablespoons butter, 2 tablespoons sugar,
1 egg, 3 tablespoons milk, 2 tablespoons jam.

CREAM THE BUTTER and sugar, beat the egg and add it to the butter and sugar. Add the flour and milk alternately. Have a greased basin ready, and put 1 tablespoon of jam in the bottom, then half the mixture. Spread over it another tablespoon of jam, then the rest of the mixture. Cover with greased paper and steam for 2 hours. Serve with milk sauce or custard.

MELTING MOMENTS

125 g butter, 60 g icing sugar,
60 g cornflour, 60 g SR flour.

Icing

1 dessertspoon icing sugar, 1 dessertspoon butter,
1 dessertspoon condensed milk,
½ teaspoon vanilla essence.

CREAM TOGETHER the butter and sugar. Add the cornflour and flour sifted together. Force through a bag or drop small pieces on a greased flat tin. Bake in a warm oven (180°C) for 10–15 minutes; do not allow to brown. When cold, join 2 together with the icing.

PEACH MELBA — ORIGINAL RECIPE

4–5 firm, ripe peaches, 300 ml raspberry syrup, vanilla
essence, 125 g sugar, 300 ml vanilla ice cream.

HALVE AND PEEL the peaches. Add the vanilla to the syrup and dissolve the sugar in it. Poach the peaches in the syrup until tender but not broken. Drain the peaches and allow them to get cold. Serve them piled around a mound of vanilla ice cream in a silver dish. Pour over a chilled, rich raspberry syrup. Serve at once.

PEACH MELBA — SIMPLE VERSION

vanilla ice cream, halved canned peaches, 1 cup
raspberry purée, sweetened whipped cream.

ALLOW 1 SCOOP of ice cream and 1 peach half per person. Place ice cream and peach halves in individual sundae glasses or dishes. Coat with raspberry purée and top with whipped cream.

The man who borrows trouble
thereby places a mortgage
on his peace of mind.

Advice is like castor oil —
easy enough to give,
but dreadful uneasy to take.

PEACH SNOWBALLS

500 g rice, some sugar, 6 peaches.

PUT THE RICE in a saucepan of boiling water and boil for 5–7 minutes. Drain, and when cool spread it in equal parts on six small pudding cloths. Peel the peaches carefully, coat them thickly with sugar and place one in the centre of each layer of rice; gather the cloth around the bundle and tie it securely. Plunge the puddings into boiling water and cook for about 1½ hours. When cooked turn them out, sprinkle with sugar and serve with a sweet sauce.

POUND CAKE

500 g SR flour, 500 g butter, 500 g fruit, 500 g sugar,
8 eggs, salt, lemon essence.

PREPARE OVEN and tin. Sift the dry ingredients and beat the eggs. Cream the butter and sugar, and add the eggs and essence gradually. Fold in the flour and fruit alternately. Place in a tin and bake in a moderate oven (200°C) for 1¾–2 hours.

POVERTY CAKE

1 cup milk, 1 cup sugar, 1 tablespoon treacle or golden
syrup, ½ tablespoon butter, 2½ cups SR flour,
1 cup raisins, nutmeg.

BEAT BUTTER and sugar together well, then add treacle or golden syrup, then the milk. Then add the remaining ingredients. Bake at 200°C.

Passionfruit Flummery

1 tablespoon gelatine, 2 cups cold water, ½ cup sugar,
1 tablespoon plain flour, juice of 2 oranges, juice of
1 lemon, 6 passionfruit, custard or whipped cream.

SOAK GELATINE in 1 cup of the cold water for 2 hours. Add sugar. Blend the flour with the remaining cup of cold water; add juice from the oranges and lemon. Put the mixture into a large saucepan and bring to the boil. Remove from the heat and, when nearly cold, add the passionfruit pulp. Beat thoroughly until thick and white. Serve very cold with custard or whipped cream.

Queensland Slice

100 g dried apricots, ¾ cup sugar, 1 tablespoon chopped
nuts, 1 cup SR flour, salt, 1 tablespoon cocoa, ½ cup
milk, 2 tablespoons butter, 1 egg, 1 tablespoon preserved
ginger, ½ cup cornflour, cinnamon,
1 tablespoon chopped chocolate.

SOAK THE APRICOTS in boiling water for 30 minutes. Drain and chop. Cream the butter and sugar, add the eggs and beat well. Fold in the nuts, ginger and apricots and mix well. Add the sifted flour, salt and cocoa alternately with the milk. Add the chocolate. Spread in a greased Swiss roll tin and bake 25–30 minutes. When cool top with the following:

Topping

2 cups icing sugar, 2 tablespoons cocoa, 1 teaspoon
coffee essence, water, 12 chopped marshmallows.

SIFT THE ICING SUGAR and cocoa into a basin. Mix in the coffee essence and enough water to obtain a spreading consistency. Mix in the marshmallows. Spread over the top and allow to set.

Rhubarb Toffee Pudding

1 tablespoon brown sugar, 250 g pastry, 500 g rhubarb,
chopped, 100 g brown sugar, ½ teaspoon ginger.

BUTTER A PUDDING BASIN thickly and sprinkle a tablespoon of
brown sugar over the butter, pressing it in. Roll out the pastry
and line the basin. Put in half the rhubarb, brown sugar, the rest
of the rhubarb and the ginger. Top with the pastry, tie greased
paper over the basin and bake for 2 hours in a moderate oven
(200°C). Turn out the pie on a hot dish.

Rice Pudding

60 g rice, pinch of salt, 30 g sugar, 2 cups milk, nutmeg,
½ cup water.

WASH THE RICE three times and leave to soak in ½ cup water for
at least 1 hour. Put in a greased pie dish with the other
ingredients and cook in a slow oven (150°C) until the rice is
done. Sago or tapioca may be used instead of rice.

ROCK CAKES

375 g SR flour, 500 g butter, 2 tablespoons fruit,
½ tablespoon peel, salt, nutmeg, 3 tablespoons sugar,
1 tablespoon almonds, 1 egg.

PREPARE OVEN and tray. Sift the dry ingredients. Prepare the fruit, peel and almonds. Cream the butter and sugar and add the beaten egg. Fold in the flour and fruit alternately. Drop the mixture in lumps on to a tray and bake for about 15 minutes in a moderate oven (200°C).

SCRIPTURE CAKE

3½ cups SR flour, 3 cups sugar, 1 cup butter, 6 eggs,
1 cup water, 1 tablespoon honey, 2 cups raisins,
2 cups figs, 1 cup almonds, mixed spice.

CREAM THE BUTTER and sugar. Add the well-beaten eggs, then the water, dry ingredients and fruit. Bake in a moderate oven (180°C) for 3 hours.

SHEARERS' PUDDING

1 cup SR flour, 1 cup breadcrumbs, ¾ cup sugar, pinch
salt, 2 tablespoons butter, ¾ cup sultanas, ½ cup
currants, 1 apple, grated, 1 banana, sliced, 1 egg, beaten,
1 tablespoon golden syrup, ⅓ cup boiling water.

RUB THE BUTTER into the flour and breadcrumbs. Dissolve the
syrup in the boiling water. Add all the remaining ingredients to
the flour and butter mixture. Place the mixture in a floured cloth
and boil for 2½–3 hours.

SPICE CAKE

375 g flour, 250 g currants, 250 g sultanas, 125 g candied
peel, 125 g butter, 125 g sugar, 2 teaspoons mixed spice,
nutmeg, 1 teaspoon powdered ginger, 2 eggs, milk.

RUB THE BUTTER into the flour, then add the spices, sugar, fruit
and candied peel. Beat the eggs with some milk and add to fruit
and spice mixture; mix well. Pour into a well-buttered tin and
bake in a moderate oven (200°C).

SUMMER PUDDING

sliced bread, milk, fresh fruit, sugar, cream or custard.

LINE A PUDDING BASIN with thin slices of bread (not fresh). Every
part of the basin must be well covered. Moisten the bread with a
little milk or cream to enable it to stick to the basin if necessary.
Boil any kind of fresh fruit with sugar until well cooked and
then pour whole into the basin. Cover with a plate, leave until
the next day, then turn out carefully. Serve with cream or
custard.

TREACLE TART

Pastry
1 cup flour (half plain and half SR), 75 g butter,
lemon juice, 1 tablespoon water.

Filling
½ cup golden syrup, grated rind of 1 lemon, lemon juice,
1 cup fresh white breadcrumbs, ½ teaspoon ground
ginger, 1 egg.

MAKE PASTRY in the usual way, then roll out and line an 18 cm tart plate. Allow the pastry to rest while you make the filling. Combine all ingredients for filling and pour into pastry case. Spread evenly, then bake in a hot oven (220°C) for 15 minutes. Reduce oven to moderate (200°C) and cook a further 15 minutes or until filling is firm to the touch.

PAVLOVA

3 egg whites, 3 tablespoons castor sugar, salt,
1 teaspoon vinegar, vanilla.

HAVE A PREPARED sandwich tin ready. Sift the castor sugar. Beat the egg whites to a very stiff froth. Add a pinch of salt and half the sugar and beat again until very stiff. Fold in the remaining sugar and trickle in the vinegar; stir lightly. Place greaseproof paper on the back of a sandwich tin. Place the mixture on the paper and form into a well-shaped round. Bake in a slow oven (150°C) for 1–1½ hours. Remove from the oven. Turn upside down on a serving plate and peel off the paper. When cold, decorate with whipped cream and any of the following: sliced banana, passionfruit, fruit salad, strawberries, orange slices, angelica, chopped nuts, crystallised cherries.

Australian Household Companion

TRIFLE

1 stale sponge cake *or* 6 small sponge cakes,
2 tablespoons raspberry jam, 2 bananas, lemon juice,
3 tablespoons fruit juice *or* sweet sherry, 1 cup warm
custard, ½ cup cream, 1 cup jelly, 6 walnuts.

SPREAD THE CAKE or cakes with jam. Slice the bananas and dip them in lemon juice. Cut the cake into slices and put into a deep glass dish, with sliced bananas between the layers. Pour the fruit juice or sherry over the sponge and, when it has soaked in, completely cover with the custard. Allow to cool thoroughly, then decorate with whipped cream, chopped jelly and chopped nuts.

WEST INDIAN CAKE

500 g flour, salt, nutmeg, 1 cup milk, 500 g mixed fruit,
½ teaspoon soda, 250 g butter, 250 g brown sugar, 2
eggs, 1 tablespoon lemon peel, vanilla and lemon essence.

PREPARE OVEN and tin. Sift the dry ingredients. Beat the eggs. Cream the butter and sugar and add the eggs gradually. Fold in the flour and fruit alternately. Place in a tin and bake for 2 hours in a moderate oven (200°C).

Gramma Tart

500 g cooked gramma or pumpkin, 1 dessertspoon butter,
1 egg yolk, 3 tablespoons sugar, juice and rind of 1 lemon,
mixed spice, 1 tablespoon sultanas or raisins,
rich short crust pastry using 250 g flour.

STEAM OR BOIL gramma (or pumpkin) in very little water until tender, then strain. Beat with a fork until smooth. Add other ingredients and mix well. Roll out the pastry and line an 18 cm tart dish with half the pastry. Place the prepared mixture in the dish and cover with the remaining pastry. Glaze with water and sugar. Bake in a hot oven (220°C) for 20 minutes. Sprinkle with icing sugar.

High Church Pudding

250 g SR flour, 90 g butter, 1 cup raspberry jam, 1 cup
milk.

MIX THE FLOUR and butter well, then add the jam and milk. Steam for 3 hours and serve with sauce.

Rice Muffins

1 cup boiled rice, 1 cup sweet milk, 2 eggs, well beaten,
5 tablespoons melted butter, salt, 1 tablespoon sugar,
1½ cups flour.

ADD THE RICE to the flour, add a pinch of salt, stir in the eggs and milk, then the butter. Beat well. Bake in hot gem irons or muffin tins in a hot oven (250°C).

Life is mostly froth and bubble;
Two things stand like stone:
Kindness in another's trouble,
Courage in your own.

SHORTBREAD

1 kg flour, 500 g butter, 250 g sugar, 1 egg.

CREAM THE BUTTER and sugar, mix in the egg, then knead in the flour. Roll out into flat cakes, prick with a fork, place on greased paper and bake for ½ hour in a moderate oven (180°C).

TEA JELLY

600 ml milk, 2 tablespoons of tea, *or* 1 tablespoon each of green and black tea, 60 g gelatine, 6 tablespoons sugar, 4 eggs, 600 ml cream.

POUR THE BOILING MILK over the tea; allow to stand 5–10 minutes and strain through a fine cloth. Soak the gelatine in a little cold water until soft, then add it to the tea and milk with the sugar and the well-beaten eggs. Stir this over a hot plate until nearly boiling, remove from heat and allow to cool. When cold and beginning to thicken stir in the whipped cream. Pour into a mould and chill for 1–2 hours.

COFFEE JELLY

600 ml milk, 4 tablespoons coffee, 60 g gelatine, 6 tablespoons sugar, 4 eggs, 600 ml cream.

BOIL THE MILK, pour it over the coffee and the gelatine (previously soaked), cover and leave to stand a few minutes. Strain. Add the sugar and eggs, well beaten, return to the stove and stir until nearly boiling. Remove from heat and allow to cool. When nearly cold and beginning to thicken stir in the whipped cream. Pour into a mould and chill for 1–2 hours.

Bread, Loaves and Scones

BILLY FRUIT LOAF

3 cups SR flour, ½ teaspoon salt, 1 teaspoon mixed
spice, 1 tablespoon ground cinnamon, 2 tablespoons
sugar, 1 cup bran, 1 tablespoon butter, 1 tablespoon
golden syrup, milk, 1 cup mixed fruit.

MIX TOGETHER the flour, salt, spices, sugar and bran. Rub in the
butter, then add the golden syrup mixed with a little milk. Add
more milk slowly, mixing all the time, until the mixture is a soft
dough. Lastly, add the mixed fruit. Place the mixture in a
greased and floured 3 pint (2 litre) billy. Put on the lid and bake
for 1½ hours (or less) in the ashes or in the oven at about
180°C, being careful not to burn the loaf.

BILLY WHOLEMEAL

2 cups wholemeal flour, 2 cups SR flour, ¾ cup sugar,
1 cup sultanas and nuts, salt, milk.

MIX THE FLOUR, sugar, fruit and salt to a soft dough with milk.
Cook in a greased and floured billy with the lid on in the very
moderate heat of the ashes or the oven — 180°C.

COUNTRY SCONES

60 g butter, 375 g SR flour, 50 g castor sugar,
50 g sultanas, 300 ml sour milk, 2 eggs.

SIFT THE FLOUR. Add the butter and sugar, mixing well. Add the sultanas and mix in the egg and milk. Knead lightly and roll out thickly. Makes about 8 large scones. Bake large ones for 10–15 minutes at 250°C; smaller ones for 8 minutes.

DAMPER—COOKED IN AN OVEN

4 cups SR flour, 2 level teaspoons salt,
1 level tablespoon sugar, ¾ cup milk, ¾ cup water,
beaten egg and milk to glaze.

SIFT FLOUR and salt into a basin. Mix in the sugar, then make a well in the centre. Pour in the milk and water and, using a knife, mix quickly into a dough. The mixture will be very light if emptied on to a lightly greased scone tray and shaped roughly into a round loaf. Glaze with beaten egg and milk. Bake in a hot oven (220°C) for about 45 minutes or until golden.

Recipes from Grandmother's Kitchen

DROUGHT LOAF

1 cup SR flour, 1 cup bran, ½ cup sugar,
½ cup sultanas, 1 tablespoon treacle, 1 cup milk.

COMBINE ALL ingredients. Put the mixture into a billy, put the lid on and boil for about 1½ hours. When cold, serve sliced and buttered.

SHEARERS' SCONES

4 cups SR flour, ½ teaspoon nutmeg, ½ teaspoon salt,
150 g butter, ½ cup castor sugar, 1 cup currants
or chopped dates, 1 egg, 1 cup milk,
beaten egg and milk to glaze.

SIFT FLOUR, nutmeg and salt into a mixing bowl. Rub in butter. Mix in sugar and fruit. Make a well in the centre. Add egg and milk, and mix quickly into a soft scone dough. Knead lightly using extra SR flour. Pat or roll out to about 2 cm thick and cut out. Put on to a greased baking tray. Glaze tops with beaten egg and milk. Bake in a very hot oven (250°C) for about 15 minutes.

Australian Household Companion

Johnny Cakes

250 g SR flour, salt, 125 g butter, 5 tablespoons milk.

SIFT THE DRY INGREDIENTS. Rub in the butter and mix in the milk. Turn out on to a floured board and knead slightly. Roll out fairly thin. Cut and cook on a hot, floured pan or girdle. Turn when brown. Serve with jam, honey or golden syrup.

Pumpkin Scones

2 cups wholemeal SR flour, salt, 2 tablespoons melted butter, 1 cup cooked and mashed pumpkin, currants or sultanas (optional), 1 tablespoon honey, 1 teaspoon cinnamon, milk, egg yolk (optional).

TO OBTAIN THE QUANTITY of mashed pumpkin, boil 250–375 g trimmed pumpkin in a little water in a covered pan for 20 minutes. Drain thoroughly and mash well. Mix all other ingredients together before adding flour. Work in a little milk to form a soft dough. Knead lightly and place scones on a greased tray. Brush with milk or milk and beaten egg yolk. Cook in a preheated oven at 200°C for 12–15 minutes until nicely browned.

Gems

250 g SR flour, ½ teaspoon salt, 30 g butter, 6 drops vanilla essence, 30 g sugar, 1 egg, 1 cup milk.

PREPARE AND HEAT OVEN and gem irons (or muffin tins). Sift dry ingredients. Cream butter and sugar, and add the beaten egg. Mix well. Add the milk and essence, then the flour. Half fill the very hot greased gem irons. Bake for 10 minutes at 220°C. Serve buttered hot or cold.

NUT BREAD

2 cups SR wholemeal flour, ½ teaspoon salt,
1 tablespoon butter, ½ cup sugar, ½ cup nuts,
1 egg, 1 cup milk.

SIFT FLOUR and salt. Rub butter into flour; add the dry ingredients. Beat the egg well and add to the milk. Add to the mixture and mix well together. The mixture must be rather wet. This bread cooks nicely in a billy with the lid on; grease both the billy and the lid. Alternatively, use a loaf tin. Bake for nearly 1 hour in a moderate oven (200°C). This loaf may also be made with dates or half nuts and half dates. Best eaten when a day old.

WHOLEMEAL BREAD

1.5 kg wholemeal flour, 3 teaspoons salt, 1 teaspoon
sugar, 30 g yeast, 60 g butter, 1 litre warm water.

MIX SALT WELL with flour and make warm in a large basin. Cream the yeast with the sugar, add the warm water, together with the melted butter, and mix with the flour to an elastic dough. Knead well until smooth, cover with a cloth and set in a warm place to rise to double its size—about 1 hour. When the dough is sufficiently risen it will have a honeycombed appearance. Knead a second time and continue until, when the dough is cut, there are no large holes in it, but do not knead too heavily. Divide into the required number of loaves. Place in warm greased tins, making the tops round. Prick and allow to prove or recover for 20 minutes, or until the dough is well up to the top of the tin. Bake in top middle of a very hot oven (230°C) for 10–15 minutes, then reduce heat to fairly hot (200°C), baking in all for about 1 hour. When ready the loaf should have a hollow sound when knocked on the bottom and should be well risen and nicely browned with a crisp crust.

Jams and Preserved Fruits

APRICOT CHUTNEY

1.5 kg apricots, 375 g sugar, 250 g preserved ginger, chopped, 2 large onions, chopped, 2 cups vinegar.

MIX ALL INGREDIENTS together and boil until the mixture thickens.

APRICOT CONSERVE

500 g stoned, underripe apricots, juice of 1 lemon,
1 cup water, 500 g sugar.

CRACK HALF THE STONES of the apricots and add the kernels to the fruit. Boil the lemon juice, water and sugar together for 10 minutes. Skim well, then put in the fruit and kernels. Boil gently for about 45 minutes or until a little sets when put on a plate to cool. Transfer to dry, heated glasses or pots. Cover immediately and store in a cool, dry place. Peaches may be substituted for apricots but use 375 g sugar to each 500 g fruit, omitting the kernels and adding ¼ teaspoon salt.

CUMQUAT CONSERVE

500 g cumquats, salt, 500 g sugar.

WASH FRUIT, put in a saucepan and cover with water. Add a handful of salt. Cook gently until tender. Drain off water. Cover with fresh water and leave overnight. Drain well next morning. Make a syrup with sugar and just enough water to moisten. Bring to the boil, add fruit and boil quickly until it jells (about 1 hour). The jam should be watched carefully or it might boil over. Bottle and seal.

FEIJOA JAM

2 kg feijoas, 2 kg sugar, 1 cup water, 1 lemon.

PEEL THE FRUIT with a potato peeler, slice it, place fruit and water in a pan and simmer for 15 minutes. Add the sugar and the juice and rind of the lemon, stir until boiling, then boil for 15 minutes.

GUAVA JELLY

2 kg red guavas, sugar, lemon juice.

WASH GUAVAS and remove their tops. Cover with cold water and simmer gently for 2 hours, then strain through a jelly bag. Measure the syrup when cold, and to each 600 ml allow 375 g sugar and 1 tablespoon lemon juice. Return to the preserving pan and boil for about 1 hour, or until a little of the syrup poured on to a cold plate jells quickly. Turn into pots, cover quickly and store.

MARROW JAM

1.5 kg old vegetable marrow, 1.5 kg sugar,
2 lemons, sliced, 50 g ginger.

DICE THE MARROW, and add the sugar, lemons and ginger. Boil the mixture until it becomes a dark colour, adding water if it seems dry.

MELON AND PINEAPPLE JAM

1 pie or snow melon

For every 2 kg of melon, allow:

1 pineapple, 1 large lemon, 375 g sugar per 500 g of fruit,
60 g ginger.

CUT UP THE MELON, pineapples and lemons, and add half the sugar. Allow to stand overnight. Next day put the mixture on to boil slowly, and when the lemon peel is soft put in the rest of the sugar. Boil until clear.

Spiced Peaches

12 peaches, 4 kg sugar, 1 tablespoon fresh ginger, mace,
cloves, white peppercorns, 1 cup vinegar.

WIPE THE DOWN OFF the peaches. Slice the ginger. Simmer all
ingredients together slowly with plenty of water until a straw
will enter the fruit, then take them out of the pan and add a cup
of vinegar to the syrup. Boil for 10 minutes and pour over the
peaches when cool.

Stewed Prickly Pears

sugar, water, prickly pears, lemon peel, lemon juice.

MAKE A SYRUP of sugar with a little water, and while boiling put
in the pears, either peeled or unpeeled. Add a few pieces of
lemon peel and the juice of a lemon. Boil the mixture until the
pears are soft but not broken. Put the fruit in a deep dish. Add a
little more sugar to the syrup, bring it to the boil and pour it over
the pears. The pears are best eaten cold with whipped cream.

Tomato Jam

6 kg ripe tomatoes, 3 kg sugar, 6 ripe apples,
1 wine glass pineapple essence.

CUT THE TOMATOES into quarters and squeeze the juice and seeds
out; then boil them until tender in just enough water to cover
them. Add the sugar and the apples, peeled, cored and chopped.
Boil in an enamel pan for 1 hour. When nearly cold add the
essence and stir well. When cold put in jars and tie down.

PRICKLY PEAR JELLY

1.5 kg prickly pears, 1.5 litres water, lemons, sugar.

RUB THE SPINES OFF the prickly pears with a thick cloth. Cut the fruit in half, put it into a pan and add the water. Boil until the fruit is almost a pulp. Strain the liquid through several layers of muslin. Do not force it; allow it to strain overnight. Then, allowing the juice of 1 lemon and 500 g sugar per 500 ml of fruit, simmer gently until the syrup jells when tested. Remove the scum as it rises. Transfer to heated jars, cover and store.

GREEN FIG JAM OR CONSERVE

---

1 kg figs, 1 kg sugar, 170 ml water, 3 tablespoons
lemon juice *or* vinegar.

WIPE AND SLICE the fruit. Boil the sugar, water and lemon juice or vinegar for 10 minutes. Add the figs to the syrup and boil gently for 1 hour, or until the jam sets when a little is put on a plate to cool. Transfer to hot, dry jars, cover and when cold store in a cool dry place.

Sauces and Dressings

BIGARADE SAUCE

2 oranges, 1 tablespoon butter, 1 tablespoon flour,
½ cup stock, salt and pepper, sugar, pinch salt.

GRATE OR PARE off thinly the rind of the oranges; cut into thin shreds and boil in water a few minutes. Melt the butter in a saucepan; gradually stir in the flour until it colours. Add the stock, salt, pepper and sugar. Add the rinds, stir until boiling and add the juice of the oranges. Serve with roast duck.

BOILED SALAD DRESSING

1 tablespoon butter, 1 tablespoon flour, 200 ml milk,
1 teaspoon salt, 1 teaspoon sugar, 1 teaspoon mixed
mustard, cayenne, yolk of 1 egg, 2 tablespoon vinegar.

MELT THE BUTTER, blend in the flour, add the milk and stir the mixture constantly until it boils. Add the salt, sugar, mustard, cayenne and the egg yolk. Return the mixture to the heat until the egg is just cooked and add the vinegar slowly, stirring with a wooden spoon.

Plum Sauce

3 kg plums, 6 cups vinegar, 1 dessertspoon salt,
1 dessertspoon cloves, 500 g onions, 1.5 kg sugar,
½ teaspoon cayenne, 1 dessertspoon mixed spice,
1 dessertspoon fresh ginger, crushed.

BOIL ALL INGREDIENTS together for 1 hour, then strain through a colander and bottle when cold.

Celery Sauce

white heart of a head of celery, 600 ml milk,
2 tablespoons flour, nutmeg, butter, 2 tablespoons cream.

BOIL THE CELERY in salted water until tender, drain and cut into small pieces. Make a sauce by boiling the milk with a spoonful of butter, thicken with flour, add a pinch of nutmeg, stir in the celery and lastly add the cream. Serve with chicken.

Worcester Sauce

6 cups vinegar, 1 cup treacle, 1 cup plum jam, 1 large
piece garlic (about ½ tablespoon), cloves, chillies,
1 tablespoon pepper, 1 tablespoon salt.

BOIL ALL INGREDIENTS together gently for 2½ hours, strain and
bring to the boil again.

Condensed Milk Salad Dressing

1 tablespoon condensed milk, ½ teaspoon mustard,
1 teaspoon salt, pepper, vinegar.

ADD THE MUSTARD, salt and pepper to the condensed milk. Use
vinegar to thin the mixture to the correct pouring consistency.

HONEY SALAD DRESSING

1 tablespoon honey, 4 tablespoon lemon juice, salt and
pepper, 1–2 tablespoons cream or evaporated milk.

MIX THE HONEY with the lemon juice, salt and pepper. Just before
serving mix again and add the cream or evaporated milk.

OYSTER SAUCE

1 dozen oysters, mace, lemon rind, 1 cup milk,
½ tablespoon butter, ½ tablespoon flour,
lemon juice, salt.

BEARD THE OYSTERS and place the beards, oyster liquid, mace and
lemon rind in a small saucepan. Boil for 5 minutes. Strain the
liquid off and add it to the milk. Use this to make a white sauce
with the butter and flour. Season with lemon juice and salt.
Scald the oysters by holding them in boiling water for 5 seconds.
Drain the oysters and add them to the sauce.

PARSLEY AND LEMON SAUCE

handful parsley, 1 lemon, 15 g butter, 15 g flour,
1–2 cups stock, mace, capers, 2 egg yolks.

MINCE PARSLEY FINELY and add pulp and rind of the lemon. Melt
butter in a saucepan with flour. Add parsley and lemon to stock
with a little mace and a few capers. Stir over heat and when
cooked remove from heat and add egg yolks. Then return to heat
and stir until sauce thickens. Do not allow to boil. Serve with
fish.

WEIGHTS AND MEASURES

IF YOU ARE WORKING in a simple kitchen with only basic equipment—whether a crude hut in the bush or in a flat in the city—you will find these equivalents very handy:

Liquids
2 teaspoons = 1 dessertspoon
2 dessertspoons = 1 tablespoon/15ml/½ fl oz
1 wineglass = 60 ml/2 fl oz
4 tablespoons = ½ cup/150 ml/¼ pint
1 cup = 250 ml/8 fl oz
1 pint = 600 ml/20 fl oz
4 cups = 1 litre/1 quart
4 quarts = 4.5 litres/1 gallon/8 pints

Solids
1 level tablespoon = 30 g/1 oz butter, lard,
    margarine, milk, salt, sugar or water
soft butter, size of an egg = 30 g/1 oz
soft butter, size of a walnut = 15 g/½ oz
1 cup butter = 250 g/½ lb
2 cups chopped meat = 500 g/1 lb
1 cup sugar = 250 g/½ lb
2 tablespoons flour = 30 g/1 oz
1 cup flour = 100 g/4 oz
4 level cups flour = 500 g/1 lb
2 tablespoons rice = 30 g/1 oz
4 tablespoons breadcrumbs = 30 g/1 oz
1 cup breadcrumbs = 60 g/2 oz
1 cup raisins or currants = 180 g/6 oz
4 average tomatoes = 500 g/1 lb
3 big bananas (with skins) = 500 g/1 lb
1 large egg = 50 g/2 oz

Old-fashioned Household Hints

ANTS

SLICES OF CUT LEMON strewn in the path of ants will deter them.

BACON

CUT OFF the rinds of bacon with scissors.

BORER

DISSOLVE CAMPHOR in kerosene and squirt into borer holes with a sewing machine oil can.

BRUISES ON FURNITURE

WASH INDENTED PLACES with warm water. Fold some brown paper a few times, soak in water and cover the bruises. Apply a hot iron to the paper until the moisture evaporates. Repeat if necessary.

CANDLE MAKING

TO MAKE CANDLES, take 6 parts by weight of alum to 5 parts of tallow; dissolve the alum in a little water, then melt the tallow in the alum water, stirring frequently, to clarify and harden the tallow. Before fixing the wick in the mould, dip it in turpentine; this will give a brighter light.

CARPETS

SPREAD RUGS over parts of the carpet subject to the heaviest wear.

BRIGHTEN UP faded carpets by washing them with a little ammonia mixed in warm water.

CHEESE

IF CHEESE is too fresh for fine grating, either vitamise it or rub it through a sieve, using a wooden spoon.

CHINA AND GLASS

TO PREVENT CHINA and glassware from cracking, when new, put the article in a large saucepan of cold water, in which 250 g salt is dissolved, and let it come to the boil gradually and boil for 10–15 minutes; then allow it to cool slowly.

Chopping

When chopping sticky ingredients, such as raisins, sprinkle with some of the measured flour for the recipe. This will stop them clogging.

Citrus Fruit

To remove scale from citrus fruit skins, rub with a nylon mit. Rinse well.

Curdling

Curdling may occur in cake-making when eggs are added to the creamed butter and sugar. If this happens, a little dry flour should be stirred in.

EGGS

WHEN FRYING or poaching eggs, first break them one at a time into a cup and, when transferring the egg to the pan, submerge the rim of the cup in the hot oil or water and let the egg slip slowly from it. This procedure enables you to avoid breaking the egg and keeps the white from spreading and becoming ragged.

WHEN HARD-BOILING eggs roll them around with a wooden spoon in water deep enough to cover, until boiling, to keep the yolk in the centre. Immerse in cold water immediately after cooking to prevent a dark ring forming around the yolk.

SALT AND a dash of vinegar in the water helps eggs to set more quickly when boiling or poaching.

EGG SPOONS

EGG SPOONS will lose dark stains if placed in the hot water in which the eggs were boiled.

FLOOR

SCOUR FLOORBOARDS with 1 part of slaked lime mixed with 3 parts common sand. Apply with a hard brush to destroy vermin and lighten the timber.

TO MAKE FLOOR POLISH: melt some wax candle ends (about two candles) and 250 g of shredded soap in 1 litre of boiling water. Stir well and allow to cool. When cold, add equal parts of turpentine and linseed oil and mix. Keep well covered.

FLOOR STAIN

METHOD 1: Put boiled linseed oil in a tin and add a little burned sienna to achieve the required colour. Test on a separate piece of timber. Apply to clean floorboards.

METHOD 2: Buy a large tin of floor polish (or make your own) and a tin of boot polish about half the size, either black or brown, according to the desired colour. Melt and stir the two together in an old saucepan and allow the mixture to cool. Apply generously to the floor with a stiff brush, rubbing in well. Polish it with a mop to achieve a shine. If the surface lightens in future darken it again with more of the mixture.

FRENCH BEANS

TO PRESERVE french beans, put young beans in wooden box in layers about 7 cm deep, with a thin layer of salt between each layer. Insert a fitted wooden cover into the box and put a weight on it. When the beans are wanted for use, soak them in water for a few hours, then cook them as usual.

FRUIT

LEMON JUICE sprinkled over white fruits, such as apples, pears and bananas, will prevent discolouration.

FRYING

FOR FRYING without oil, place meat in a pan in which a teaspoon of salt has been heated.

FRUIT LEATHERS

BANANA LEATHER: mash bananas and add lemon juice, the finely grated rind of the lemon and a little honey. Mix well. Spread on a tray and sun-dry.

STRAWBERRY LEATHER: Method 1. Boil 500 g sugar with 150 ml water until it threads. Put in 1 litre of clean strawberries and boil. Pour on to a tray and dry in the sun for 2–3 days. (Cherries may also be preserved this way.)

STRAWBERRY LEATHER: Method 2. Thoroughly mash ripe strawberries to a pulp. Spread on a tray and sun-dry, or put in a low oven. When dry, dust with icing sugar (optional). Roll up and keep in glass jars.

FISH

WHEN BOILING FISH add a spoonful or two of vinegar, or the juice of a lemon to the water; the acid helps to keep the fish firm.

DO NOT PUT FISH into boiling water or it will crack the skin. Only deeply coloured fish are put into boiling water to set the colour.

GRAPES

TO KEEP GRAPES: remove any imperfect grapes from bunches that are not too ripe, then lay the bunches on a layer of dry bran in a box, so that the bunches do not touch. Add a layer of bran between the layers of grapes. Cover all with bran, and make the box airtight.

INSECT REPELLENT

LAVENDER in the linen cupboard or sewn into the hems of curtains will repel insects.

TO MAKE a natural pest spray: crush 100 g garlic and pour 2 teaspoons paraffin oil over it. Cover and soak for 48 hours. Then make a pure soap solution, say 30 g soap powder in 600 ml of hot water. Pour it over the garlic and mix. Leave for 24 hours, then warm slightly and strain. Bottle and label the bottle. Use 1 part in 100 parts of water, or less, depending on the problem.

INK AND MILDEW

TO REMOVE ink stains or mildew from white cloths, rub with lemon and salt, and then wash.

LEMON

A FEW DROPS of lemon juice added to water when washing will make glass shine, whiten rice and separate the grains when cooking and will remove stains from porcelain.

Two's company—three's everything.

LEMON JUICE

TO KEEP LEMON JUICE: squeeze the lemons, strain the juice through fine muslin and put the juice into very small bottles, leaving about 3 cm at the top. Fill the remaining space with salad oil and cork tightly. When you want to use the lemon juice, remove the oil with a piece of cotton wool.

MARINADE

MARINADE MEATS for better flavour. Equal parts of oil and wine or vinegar, with chopped herbs and spices, and a little chopped onion or garlic if desired, makes a good marinade. Meat for grills, kebabs and cold meat dishes benefit from marinading.

MARINADE FOR LAMB SHANKS

MAKE SLITS in the shank and insert pieces of fresh garlic. Use fresh herbs, beer or yoghurt (enough to cover the meat), tamari or soy sauce, peppers, 1 tablespoon of mustard and 1 glass of wine (optional) to make a marinade. Allow the meat to sit in the mixture for as long as possible—even as much as 24 hours.

MIXING

MIX PASTRY and scones with a knife, puddings with a spoon.

ALWAYS STIR before you pour.

BEAT a curdled custard with an egg beater.

Old Clothes and Linen

USE UP WORN GARMENTS by making them into quilts or rag rugs. Worn tablecloths can be turned into napkins for everyday use. Worn sheets can be cut down the middle and restitched with a flat seam to prolong their useful lives.

Paint

TO REMOVE OLD PAINT and varnish from woodwork, apply a mixture of 2 parts ammonia and 1 part turpentine. This emulsion will soften the paint so that it can be scraped or rubbed off after a few moments.

Parsley

CUT UP PARSLEY with a pair of scissors.

PASTRY

WHEN PLACING one layer of pastry on top of another, one of the layers must be moistened so that the layers will stick together.

PORRIDGE

PORRIDGE WILL COOK more quickly if the oats are soaked overnight beforehand.

POTATOES

TO PRESERVE POTATOES, dip them for 1–2 minutes in boiling water. They will last about a year.

POURING

WHEN ABOUT TO POUR anything hot into a glass dish, first place a spoon or fork in the dish as this prevents cracking.

PRICKLY PEARS

GATHER RIPE FRUIT and put them in a tub of hot water. Stir them roughly to get rid of some of the little prickles. Rub off the rest of the prickles with a thick cloth. The fruit can be eaten raw but is very good stewed.

Rabbit

IF A RABBIT IS FRESH, the body will be stiff, the flesh white and dry in appearance. Stale rabbits can be slimy with a bluish tinge to the flesh. The meat of the rabbit is delicate but tends to be rather dry and therefore is best cooked with bacon to add a little fat to the meat.

Rags

MAKE DISHCLOTHS or rags out of old underwear. Cotton T-shirts are especially soft and make excellent dusters or polishing cloths.

Rugs

STITCH A SMALL PIECE of rubber from an old car inner tube or an old hot-water bottle under each corner of a rug to prevent slipping on a polished floor.

Salt

SALT, WHEN COOKED with meat, brings out the juices. Therefore, it may be used in stews and casserole dishes, but not when boiling or roasting meat.

Scratches on Furniture

MIX EQUAL PARTS of linseed oil and turpentine. Dip a flannel into the mixture and rub well into the scratched parts. Polish with a soft duster and the scratches will become almost invisible.

Soap Making

To MAKE SOAP, add 1.5 kg quicklime (shell lime is best) and 1.5 kg washing soda to 5.5 litres of water. Boil for 30 minutes; let it stand all night to clear. Draw off the lye and add to it 250 g common resin and 1.5 kg of any fat. Boil this for 30 minutes, leave until cool and cut into bars.

Soup

To GET RID OF excess salt in soup, add a slice of peeled, raw potato. Boil for a few minutes, then remove the potato.

To REMOVE FAT from the top of soup, use blotting paper, tissues or paper towels. If the soup is cold, use a spoon to remove the congealed fat.

To MAKE A BOUQUET GARNI for soup, tie together sprigs of various fresh herbs or wrap them in a muslin bag. Immerse the bouquet garni in the soup during cooking and remove before serving.

SPONGE CAKES

TO PREVENT SPONGE CAKES from sticking, grease or oil the tin and dust with equal parts of cornflour and castor sugar.

SPRAY

TO MAKE A freshening spray for rooms, mix the juice of 1 lemon with 1 litre of strong tea. Strain and store in an old spray bottle.

STOCK

FOR A CLEAR STOCK, do not brown meat or vegetables. Use the white and shell of an egg. Whisk over the heat. Boil for half an hour; this removes any impurities. Always clear stock the day it is to be used.

STUFFING

AN APPLE ADDED to sage and onion stuffing both adds to the flavour and prevents the onion repeating.

TOMATOES

TOMATOES CAN BE PEELED more readily if first dropped in boiling water.

CLEANING WALLPAPER

REMOVE GREASE SPOTS on wallpaper by rubbing gently with a soft flannel sprinkled with plaster of Paris, Fuller's earth or borax. Clean small sections at a time, rubbing downwards with even strokes. An art gum rubber will remove pencil marks. You could also try using slices of stale bread or the inside of a loaf of stale bread, rubbing evenly and slicing off the outside of the bread as it gets dirty.

WINDOW CLEANING

USE A WAD OF NEWSPAPER to apply wet polish to windows and mirrors. Dry sheets of newspaper give a better shine than any cloth.

METHOD 1: Use a cloth or wad of newspaper wrung out to which 1 tablespoon vinegar or methylated spirits has been added. Rub off and shine with sheets of clean newspaper.

METHOD 2: Add 2 tablespoons of ammonia to 1 litre of water. Apply with a cloth or squirt from a reused plastic bottle.

Sweeping

SAVE USED TEA LEAVES and sprinkle generously over polished floors. Dust and fluff will cling to the damp leaves and can be swept up easily, leaving floors nice and clean, and no dust in the atmosphere.

Removing Wallpaper

USE SUGAR SOAP (also known as painter's soap) and mix as instructed on the packet. Wet the wallpaper thoroughly and remove it in strips. Use a scraper at the edges and corners. (This method does not work with vinyl wallpapers.)

Weevils

A FEW BAY LEAVES taped to the lid of a food container will make weevils disappear. To make them leave stores of dried fruit, add a twist of lemon rind to the jar.

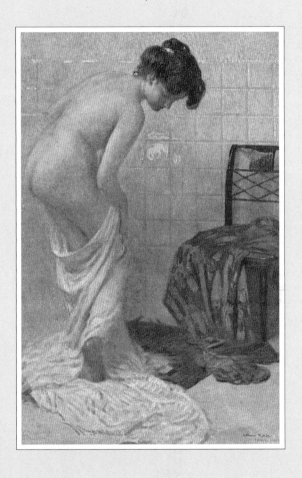

Natural Home Remedies

ACHES AND PAINS

To RELIEVE NEURALGIA, a cold or earache, cut up young gum leaves very finely, mix them with some cooking oil or water and boil for a few minutes. Then pour the mixture into a handkerchief or a woollen sock; hold this against the affected part and relief will follow in a minute or two.

ACNE

THE JUICE OF PARSLEY, extracted by sieving the leaves, will fix acne or boils if applied to the affected area.

ALOE

ALOE IS A REMEDY for bites, rashes, ringworm, ulcers, blisters, cuts, burns and scratches. Its juice also heals sunburn. Having your own aloe plant is well worth while.

CRYING BABIES

DILUTED CAMOMILE TEA will soothe babies with teething troubles or stomach ache.

BEEF TEA

SHRED 500 g rump steak finely and place in a jar with some salt, 1 cup water and 1 teaspoon lemon juice. Stand the jar, with lid on, in a saucepan of boiling water. Cook gently for 3–4 hours.

QUICK BEEF TEA

SHRED 500 g rump steak finely and add some salt, 1 cup water and 1 teaspoon lemon juice. Allow to stand for ½ hour. Heat very slowly until the liquid turns brown. Do not allow to boil. Strain and serve with sippets of toast.

BITES

EQUAL QUANTITIES of cold tea and methylated spirits will ease the itching of an insect bite almost immediately.

BLISTERS AND SUNBURN

TO SOOTHE BLISTERS and relieve sunburn make and apply the following remedy: combine ¼ cup cornstarch, ¼ cup plain talcum powder, ¼ cup rice flour, 1 teaspoon boric acid powder and 3 drops vanilla extract. Store in a lidded tin in a cool, dry place.

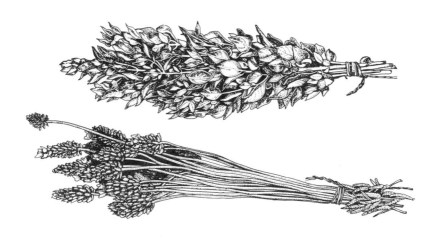

FRESH BREATH

TO FRESHEN YOUR BREATH, try chewing fennel seeds, rosemary or caraway. Even better is chewing a few parsley leaves or rinsing your mouth with a tea made with parsley.

BROWN PATCHES

BROWN PATCHES on the back of your hands can be faded by rubbing in a crushed vitamin C tablet mixed with saliva. Another remedy is to make a paste by melting either lemon juice, or the juice of a fresh leek, or pulped lettuce leaves, and beeswax together slowly. When cool apply the paste generously to your hand, leave until cold and rinse off.

BRUISING

TO REDUCE BRUISING, apply raw, peeled and grated potato.

BURNS

LAVENDER OIL will both soothe and heal household burns caused by contact with hot pans or the iron.

ALTERNATIVELY, try applying cucumber and milk blended together.

WEAK CHEST

FOR A WEAK CHEST: mix 300 ml whisky, 250 g golden syrup and 30 g pure glycerine thoroughly, pour into a bottle and take a tablespoonful two or three times a day.

CHICKEN BROTH

CUT UP 1 CHICKEN and boil for 2 hours with 6 cups water, 1 teaspoon salt, ½ tablespoon rice and 1 small onion, chopped. Strain and skim off the fat. Serve with chopped parsley.

CHILBLAINS

TO RELIEVE CHILBLAINS, pound salt and garlic together and bandage to the affected parts. Alternatives include rubbing the chilblain with a slice of onion; applying a hot poultice of turnip parings; or rubbing with slices of potato which have been salted and allow to stand overnight.

Poor Circulation

To IMPROVE poor circulation, add the following mixture to your bathwater and take a bath: steep 2 tablespoons freshly crushed ginger in boiling water and mix with witchhazel. While in the bath, rub yourself briskly with a handful of sea salt and a loofah.

Colds

To PREVENT COLDS and flu, take garlic broth. Crush 2 garlic cloves and fry gently in a little oil. Add 750 ml chicken broth and simmer for 15 minutes. Stir in 3 beaten egg yolks just before serving.

FOR A COLD, take treacle posset: put 1 cup milk on to boil, stir in 2 tablespoons treacle and continue stirring until the milk curdles. Strain finely and serve the liquid very hot. Should be taken in bed.

COUGH

TO RELIEVE A COUGH, dice an onion, cover it with golden syrup, leave for 3 hours and eat.

COUGH MIXTURE

BEAT TOGETHER 6 EGGS (including shells) and juice of 12 lemons. Let stand until shells are dissolved, then add 500 ml rum and 500 g honey. Take one tablespoon 3 times a day.

CONSTIPATION

DRINK A GLASS OF HOT WATER first thing in the morning, before breakfast. Eat one or two apples at breakfast and again at bedtime. Dried figs and prunes are also excellent.

DANDRUFF

AN EFFECTIVE, traditional remedy for dandruff: mix 1 teaspoon methylated spirits and 1 teaspoon sulphur with 2 tablespoons warmed Vaseline. Rub into the scalp thoroughly, leave overnight and wash out in the morning.

DIGESTION

AS AN AID to digestion, finish a rich spicy meal with pawpaw or pineapple.

DIARRHOEA

WASH 25 g RICE WELL in cold water, dry and put into small saucepan with 500 ml cold water and a small piece of cinnamon stick. Simmer for 1 hour, add sugar to taste and let cool. This rice water will help ease diarrhoea.

SORE EYES

TO MAKE an effective eyebath for sore eyes and prevent redness, combine 50 ml rose water, 150 ml boiled water, a handful of rose petals and a pinch of salt in a small saucepan. Simmer for 15 minutes, allow to cool and strain. Rinse your eyes with the mixture, using either an old-fashioned eye cup or your palm.

SORE FEET

RELIEVE SORE FEET by soaking them in Epsom salts dissolved in warm water.

FLATULENCE

TO RELIEVE FLATULENCE, try drinking a little cider vinegar diluted in water before each meal.

HOT FLUSHES

AN INFUSION of dried sage leaves, smoked overnight in warm water and fresh lemon juice and strained, is often helpful in treating hot flushes.

Australian Household Companion

FINGERNAILS

STAINED FINGERNAILS can be cleaned by using equal parts of sugar, lemon juice and dripping.

TO STRENGTHEN FINGERNAILS and prevent splitting, massage them with this mixture every day: 1 egg yolk, 3 teaspoons sea salt and 1 teaspoon olive oil.

THE FLU

THIS ANTISEPTIC SYRUP is rich in vitamin C and ideal for someone coming down with the flu. Pour half a bottle of blackcurrant cordial into a saucepan, add 1 tablespoon ginger and 1 teaspoon cloves and simmer over a low heat.

A HOT MUSTARD FOOTBATH will warm a clammy body and stimulate the circulation.

TO CLEAR A STUFFY NOSE and soothe a sore throat, inhale the steam from a jug of boiling water containing eucalyptus oil. Alternatively, sprinkle the oil on your pillow or handkerchief.

GARLIC

GARLIC HAS MANY PROPERTIES and is important in resisting and overcoming infections. It also reduces blood pressure. Fresh slices of garlic can be steeped for several hours in honey and taken at the first sign of a cold or flu. (Fresh parsley will help remove the odour from the breath.)

TO ELIMINATE the smell of garlic from your breath, eat a few orange segments after the meal.

Fever

GIVE A FEVERISH PATIENT apple water. Slice 3 washed, unpeeled apples and simmer until soft. Strain, add a little lemon for flavour and chill before drinking.

TO COOL A RAGING FEVER, make mint cordial by mixing mint and brown sugar with brandy. Drink a wineglass full every 3 hours.

Grazes and Scratches

FOR GRAZES and scratches apply this mixture: soak a handful of marigold flowers in brandy and store in a warm place for 2 weeks. Strain and store in a clear glass jar.

MAKE A DISINFECTANT by combining crushed garlic with a little water or vinegar.

Gruel

PUT 1 CUP MILK on to boil. Mix 1 tablespoon oatmeal with 2 tablespoons cold water. Pour the boiling milk over this mixture. Stir for 3 minutes. Strain into a saucepan and cook for 8 minutes. Serve with ½ teaspoon butter and 1 teaspoon sugar.

Chapped Hands

A PASTE for chapped hands: wash 100 g unsalted hog's lard in rosewater and mix it with 2 eggs, a large spoonful of honey and enough oatmeal or almond meal to make a paste.

To RELIEVE a headache, drink a weak tea made from dried lavender flowers and dab lavender cologne on your forehead and temples.

ALTERNATIVELY, dip the bristles of your hairbrush into a dish containing a mixture of 1 teaspoon lavender oil and a few drops of wheatgerm oil. Bend over and brush your hair from the nape of your neck to the ends with long strokes.

AT THE FIRST SIGN of a headache, take a very hot foot bath using chamomile flowers, lavender or lemon balm.

NUTMEG GRATED INTO A CUP of boiling water will often cure a violent headache.

Falling Hair

If troubled by falling hair, massage a little warm castor oil into the scalp each day.

Hiccoughs

Take 1 teaspoon brown sugar moistened with pure vinegar.

Insomnia

Chamomile tea is soothing and sleep-inducing taken at bedtime. Try sleeping on a lavender pillow.

Insect Repellent

Add pennyroyal to baby oil to repel mosquitoes, and put it in a herb bag to keep insects out of cupboards.

HONEY

HONEY DABBED on to cuts and grazes will act as a disinfectant and help the healing process. Honey will also cleanse and moisturise your face.

MUSCULAR PAIN

TO RELIEVE muscular pain, make a mustard plaster by adding tepid water and flour to mustard seeds and mixing to a thick paste. Place in a folded cloth and apply to the painful area. Juniper and eucalyptus oils combined can be rubbed on aching muscles.

NAPPY RASH

THE BEST THING for nappy rash is dried and powdered marigold flowers. The powder can be added to the baby's bathwater, or blended with Vaseline and rubbed into a sore bottom, or even used to make a calming drink for a noisy baby.

NAUSEA

TO RELIEVE NAUSEA and vomiting, steep 2 teaspoons of powdered cinnamon and ground nutmeg in boiling water for 15 minutes. Allow to cool, then sip an hour before meals.

NOSE BLEEDS

MOISTEN A SMALL PIECE of cotton wool in a solution of Friar's Balsam and put into the nostril. Very cold water may also help.

CRACKED NIPPLES

HANDFULS OF GRATED CARROT will relieve nipples cracked and sore from breastfeeding.

RED NOSES

A COMPRESS of orange juice and peel is an effective antidote to red noses.

PIMPLES

TO DRAW PIMPLES, apply a dab of either castor oil or honey twice a day.

YOU COULD ALSO TRY steeping nasturtium leaves in boiling water, straining and dabbing on the liquid.

PUFFY FACE

AN INFUSION of camomile will reduce puffiness and refine the pores if used as a facial wash.

SAGE

A TEA MADE from fresh sage will help to soothe a ticklish cough and soothe the nerves. It is also a good deodorant and, when added to bathwater, sage will stimulate tired muscles.

Dry Skin

A GRUEL MADE from oatmeal and added to your bathwater is a good remedy for dry skin and eczema, and also relieves nappy rash.

Sleep

TO ENSURE GOOD SLEEP, drink warm milk with a drop of brandy, or lime tea, or lettuce tea before going to bed. Lettuce tea can be made from the dark outer leaves. Simmer gently in water for 10 minutes before straining and drinking.

AN INFUSION of camomile will help insomniacs to sleep.

Removing Splinters

BEFORE ATTEMPTING to remove a splinter, hold an ice cube to the spot for a few minutes. This will have a numbing effect and make it much easier to remove the splinter.

Stings and Bites

To RELIEVE A BEE STING, remove the sting and then make a thick paste of baking soda and water. Plaster the paste over the bite and cover with a wet cloth. Onion juice and ammonia also work. To relieve the bite of a bull ant, apply damp salt. To heal a wasp sting, apply a mixture of honey and crushed marigold petals, or a handful of clay or wet earth.

Sunburn

To RELIEVE SUNBURN, apply cold black tea to the burned area. Then place slices of tomato to reduce the sting further. A generous application of chilled mayonnaise is also effective.

Sore Throat

To RELIEVE A SORE THROAT, gargle with a mixture of lemon juice and honey.

Toothache

A STRONG HOT SOLUTION of salt in vinegar will often give instant relief. Apply with a flannel or sponge as hot as possible.

Warts

THE MILK THAT RUNS from the stem of a thistle when you break it will make warts disappear quickly. Alternatively, try equal parts of kerosene, lemon juice and castor oil, applied three times a day for a week.

New Year's Greeting

Health and Beauty Secrets

ASTRINGENT WASH

STEEP 25 g ROSE PETALS and a handful of chamomile flowers in 2 cups of white wine vinegar for a week. Strain and add 1 cup of rose water to the liquid. Use as an astringent wash for face and body.

BATH

TO REFRESH THE BODY, add 1 cup epsom salts to a hot bath. Have some crushed ice in a facewasher to place on forehead in case you feel too hot.

BEAUTY BATH

MIX TOGETHER A HANDFUL each of lavender flowers, mint, crushed comfrey root and thyme leaves. Add 1 litre boiling water and simmer for 20 minutes. Strain and add to bath water and soak in it for at least 20 minutes.

BLACKHEADS

MIX ALMOND MEAL with a little cinnamon and make into a paste with lemon juice. Rub gently into area to remove blackheads.

A PASTE OF OATMEAL is also very good for blackheads.

BLOODSHOT EYES

MAKE A COLD INFUSION of parsley, elderflowers or eyebright and bathe the eyes; eyebright is particularly effective.

BLONDE HAIR

To keep blonde hair light and shiny, rinse with 15 g chamomile flowers boiled in 500 ml boiling water for 20 minutes and cooled.

COMPLEXION

To bring roses to your cheeks, place a handful of sultanas and 1 grated carrot in a bowl, cover with orange juice, refrigerate overnight, strain and drink.

CHAPPED HANDS

Melt 200 g vaseline with 2 litres elderflowers in a saucepan. Simmer for half an hour, then strain while very hot through muslin into small jars.

CREAMS

SIMPLE HAND CREAM: put 500 g lard in a basin and fill it with boiling water; leave to cool. Skim off the lard when it has risen to the top and repeat the process. When cold and skimmed again, whisk with a knife until it becomes creamy and smooth. Add lemon essence, or some essential oil, for perfume.

FACE CREAM: melt 1 part pure white lard in 4 parts rose oil (olive oil in which rose petals have been steeped). Pour the liquid from one container to another, adding a little cold water each time and stirring constantly. If desired, you could substitute a herbal infusion or rose water for the plain water. Add spirits of vinegar to the mixture to make the cream more readily absorbable.

HAND OR FACE CREAM: mix equal quantities of glycerine or almond oil and pure rendered (clarified) mutton fat. Add eau-de-Cologne or any favourite perfume.

A Fine Complexion

FOR A FINE COMPLEXION, take a large handful of violet flowers and pour over 150 ml of warm milk. Steep for several hours and strain, keeping the milk in a closed container in the refrigerator. Apply to the face and neck with cotton balls.

Crow's Feet

TO FIRM AND TIGHTEN the delicate skin around the eyes, where crow's feet form, apply a mixture comprising equal parts of cucumber juice, lemon juice and witchhazel.

Deodorant

MAKE NATURAL DEODORANT from a mixture of witchhazel and a few drops of essential oil.

Eye Make-up

TO REMOVE EYE MAKE-UP, use olive oil or almond oil, tissue off gently, then wash face in luke-warm water.

Elbows

TO SOFTEN AND WHITEN ELBOWS, cut a lemon in half and lean one elbow in each lemon half. Do this while reading the paper or a book!

ELBOW CREAM

A MIXTURE OF NATURAL YOGHURT, thickened cream, white wine vinegar and avocado, thoroughly blended together, will soften the hard skin of elbows and knees.

ELDERFLOWER

ELDERFLOWER LOTION will soothe sunburn, eliminate redness, fade freckles, relieve tired or reddened eyes and even make a soothing aftershave. Steep crushed, fresh elderflowers in 2 cups of boiling water for 15 minutes. Strain and store in the refrigerator.

EYES

PUFFY EYELIDS can be soothed by covering them with slices of chilled cucumber.

SLICES OF POTATO will restore the sparkle to tired eyes.

IF YOU HAVE dark circles under your eyes, try applying puréed peppermint leaves to your lids. Alternatively, dampened and chilled peppermint teabags will work just as well.

FACIAL SCRUB

TO IMPROVE a dull complexion gently scrub your skin with an oatmeal bag (oatmeal in a muslin bag). Then apply a tonic made by combining 1 tablespoon vinegar, 1 tablespoon eau-de-Cologne and almond oil.

FACE MASK

A MIXTURE OF YOGHURT, fresh cream and mashed avocado makes an excellent face mask.

FACE AND HAND LOTION

MIX 500 ml ORANGE FLOWER WATER, 12 g glycerine and ½ teaspoon powdered borax and bottle.

FRECKLES

TO FADE FRECKLES, scrape 1 tablespoon fresh horseradish into 1 cup sour milk. Let stand for 24 hours and apply to face.

Hands

COLD BOILED POTATOES used like soap will thoroughly cleanse the hands and keep the skin soft.

Highlights

TO BRING OUT the highlights in your hair, shampoo, then rinse your hair with the juice of 1 lemon strained in fine cloth added to a basin of warm water. Rinse until clean. An alternative is to soak ½–1 lemon in lukewarm water, then squeeze out the skin and discard it, and rinse your hair in the mixture after shampooing.

TO IMPART HIGHLIGHTS to hair, mix a beaten egg with a strong brew of coffee (brunettes), rosehip tea or red wine (redheads) or cooking water from boiled beetroots (blondes).

Ingrained Dirt

TO DISLODGE INGRAINED DIRT under fingernails, drag your nails through a cake of soap or dig them into a peeled lemon before scrubbing thoroughly.

Hair Lightening

TO MAKE A LIGHTENING RINSE for the hair, brew camomile flowers in white wine vinegar.

AN INFUSION OF CAMOMILE combed through hair after each shampoo and finger-dried in the sun is an effective hair lightener for fair hair.

GREYING HAIR

TO DISGUISE greying hair, try rinsing it with a strong infusion of privet leaves, or try thinly slicing the peel of 3 green oranges, steep them in fine almond oil for a fortnight, strain, comb through your hair and shampoo.

STEEP A GOOD HANDFUL of fresh sage leaves in 600 ml boiling water. Strain and cool, then pour over hair and work well into scalp with fingers. Catch rinse in a basin and repeat several times to darken greying hair.

HAIR CARE

IF YOU HAVEN'T GOT TIME to wash your hair, scrub a handful of bran or orris root powder through it and brush thoroughly.

JOJOBA OIL, poured into the palms of your hands and applied to your hair, will soften and add shine to dry, dull or damaged hair.

TO CLEAR SCALP DISORDERS and give a rich shine to dark hair, rinse your hair after shampooing in a cooled tea made from fresh sage.

TO MAKE HAIR SHINE, make sure you get plenty of vitamin B.

OILY SKIN

TO REDUCE THE SHINE of oily skin, apply cucumber juice and allow to dry.

TO BLOT AN OILY FACE on a hot day, dab with cotton balls soaked in lemon juice, witchhazel or eau-de-Cologne.

FACIAL TREATMENT

FOR A REFRESHING and cleansing facial, make a strong, hot infusion of chamomile tea. Pour into a bowl, place a towel over the head, and hold face over the liquid for 4 or 5 minutes. Then splash face with cold water.

FACE PACK

TO TONE AND CLEANSE THE SKIN: mix finely ground oatmeal to a paste with yoghurt and apply to face for 10-15 minutes. Especially good for oily skin.

FOR DRY SKIN, mashed avocado is an excellent face pack used as above.

Falling Hair

A POMADE for falling hair: mix 30 g beef marrow, 15 ml castor oil, 3 g tincture of cantharides and 12 drops each of oil of bitter almonds and lemon.

Insect Repellent

A FEW DROPS of citronella dabbed on to the skin will keep mosquitoes and sandflies at bay.

Massage Mixture

FOR A MASSAGE MIXTURE, simmer camomile flowers in oil.

Lips

TO SOFTEN THE SKIN of your lips, try rubbing in cocoa butter, Vaseline or almond oil.

Leg Colour

TO GIVE COLOUR to bare legs, soak them in strong cold tea and allow to dry without towelling.

PICK-ME-UP

To REVIVE YOURSELF after a busy day, lie down for 15–20 minutes with feet propped up high on pillows and place wet, cold, used tea bags on eyes. You will then be ready for the evening.

PIMPLES

TRY DABBING PIMPLES with undiluted, freshly squeezed lemon juice. It has an antiseptic and drying effect.

WAKING REFRESHED

AFTER A LATE NIGHT, particularly if much alcohol has been taken, drink two large glasses of water before going to bed. A good night's sleep and a clear head in the morning will result.

PARSLEY

PARSLEY HAS MANY USES. It cures bad breath, prevents flatulence, provides iron and acts as a general cleanser.

POMADE

To MAKE A POMADE: render down 250 g bone marrow in the oven. When cool, beat with a fork, adding 15 ml glycerine and a few drops of bergamot essence.

PAINT STAINS

TO REMOVE PAINT STAINS from your hands, massage them with a scrub made from raw sugar, sesame oil and lemon juice.

SETTING LOTION

TO MAKE A SETTING LOTION for your hair, mix 1 teaspoon glycerine with 6 tablespoons rose water, 1 teaspoon rectified spirit and ½ tablespoon ammonia.

SKIN CONDITION

TO SOFTEN AND WHITEN your skin, float lemon skins in the bath. Squeeze them out and rub your skin with the lemon. Lemon peel also whitens fingernails.

Skin Care

BUTTERMILK IS an excellent skin toner and can be applied to face, neck, shoulders and arms. Allow to dry, then rinse off. Furthermore, milk is a good cleanser; butter is good for roughened skin; and yoghurt and whey may both be used to whiten the complexion.

TO REDUCE ENLARGED PORES and clear blackheads, massage castor sugar gently into your skin with a clean face flannel, or try a chopped fresh tomato, also applied with a flannel. Then rub in a massage oil made of camomile and lavender oils blended together and gently smoothed in; leave overnight.

FOR A SIMPLE and effective skin cleansing treatment, pour boiling water into a bowl, add grated lemon rind, parsley and mint leaves or a handful of rose petals to the water, then lean over and inhale the steam.

TO CLEANSE YOUR SKIN, place ½ cup violet flowers in a bowl and heat 500 ml of milk, stirring constantly. Pour the milk over the flowers and allow to stand 1 hour. Strain, bottle and refrigerate. Pat your face twice a day with cottonwool balls soaked in the milk.

Sweet Breath

MAKE A PASTE OF MINT, orange and honey as a breath sweetener.

Toenails

FOR DRY, CRACKED TOENAILS, massage wheatgerm oil into nails and cuticles.

Skin Tonic

FOR A SOOTHING and refreshing skin tonic, mix equal quantities of witchhazel and lemon grass, and simmer for 5 minutes. Stand over the steam to open the pores of your skin. Then apply a witchhazel and white wine vinegar to your face.

TO MAKE A ROSE-scented skin toner, bruise a handful of pink rose petals and soak them in a saucer of rose water. Press the petals over your face and neck, then leave for 10 minutes. After removing them, wipe away any residue with a damp cotton ball.

White Hair

YELLOWISH STAINS in white hair can be toned down with the following elderberry mixture. Crush a handful of elderberries, add 1 teaspoon salt and 1 teaspoon alum, mix with water and bring to the boil. Add enough water to make a creamy paste. Allow to cool and apply to hair. Cover with plastic or a shower cap and wrap in a hot towel. Leave for 30 minutes and shampoo.

Yellow Teeth

YELLOW TEETH can be whitened by rubbing with lemon peel or sage leaves.

Favourites from our Household

Australian Household Companion

....
....
....
....
....
....
....
....
....
....
....
....
....
....
....
....

Favourites from Our Household

....
....
....
....
....
....
....
....
....
....
....
....
....
....
....
....
....
....
....
....
....
....
....
....

Australian Household Companion

....
....
....
....
....
....
....
....
....
....
....
....
....
....
....
....
....
....
....
....
....

Favourites from Our Household

....
....
....
....
....
....
....
....
....
....
....
....
....
....
....
....
....
....
....
....
....
....
....
....

Australian Household Companion

....
....
....
....
....
....
....
....
....
....
....
....
....
....
....
....
....
....
....
....
....
....
....
....
....
....
....

Favourites from Our Household

A Family Library Book
487 Maroondah Highway, PO Box 257
Ringwood, Victoria 3134, Australia

Copyright © Penguin Books Australia 1992

Compiled by Cathryn Game

ISBN 0 670 90589 5

Printed in Australia by Griffin Press,
Netley, South Australia